"Pure O" OCD

Letting Go of Obsessive Thoughts with Acceptance & Commitment Therapy

CHAD LEJEUNE, PHD

New Harbinger Publications, Inc.

Publisher's Note

NEW HARBINGER PUBLICATIONS is a registered trademark of New Harbinger Publications, Inc.

New Harbinger Publications is an employee-owned company.

Copyright © 2023 by Chad LeJeune
New Harbinger Publications, Inc.
5720 Shattuck Avenue
Oakland, CA 94609
www.newharbinger.com

FSC
www.fsc.org
MIX
Paper | Supporting responsible forestry
FSC® C008955

Cover design by Amy Shoup

Acquired by Jess O'Brien

Edited by Rona Bernstein

Library of Congress Cataloging-in-Publication Data on file

Printed in the United States of America

26   25   24

10   9   8   7   6   5   4   3

"'Pure O' is getting more attention, finally, and Chad LeJeune's book will be a part of the shift in understanding it. Acceptance and commitment therapy (ACT) works for obsessive-compulsive disorder (OCD) because it helps us create a new relationship with our thoughts, and the ability to unhook from the stickiness of them. LeJeune guides the reader through this process of defusing from the content of their thoughts, and toward a values-led life."

—**Stuart Ralph**, counseling and psychotherapist for children and
young people, and host of *The OCD Stories* podcast

"Some thoughts can become so sticky that they begin to run our lives: Thoughts about disgusting things; possible inadequacies; future losses or betrayals; harm to others. Often the mental adjustments we make to diminish them only make them more central—creating the neurobiological equivalent of ruts in a well-traveled dirt road. This book confronts that system head-on and provides an evidence-based pathway forward.

Don't target the thoughts; target the stickiness. Step by step, this book teaches you how to do that, with creative exercises focused on five readily learned skills. If you are living inside this torment, this book will help show you how to take your life back. Sure-footed, kind, and very well written, you will know immediately that you are in the experienced hands of a world-class expert in 'Pure O' who can teach you life-changing skills. I can highly recommend it."

—**Steven C. Hayes, PhD**, Nevada Foundation Professor in the
department of psychology at the University of Nevada, Reno;
author of A *Liberated Mind*; and originator of ACT

"When thinking about OCD, most people quickly think about germs, contamination, cleanliness, or orderliness. Yet for those suffering from OCD, there are so many ways in which their brain latches onto obsessions. 'Pure O' is the theme that captures those obsessions and compulsions that are invisible to the eyes of others, but highly distressing to the person having them. LeJeune will show you how to understand those sticky thoughts (through the characters Anthony, Sophie, and Lou), and how you can use ACT to tackle those particular OCD episodes through the five microskills embedded in the acronym: LLAMP. This is a must-read book for anyone dealing with OCD and thought-based compulsions in particular, and who wants to experience rich and fulfilling connections!"

—**Patricia E. Zurita Ona, PsyD**, author of *Acceptance and
Commitment Skills for Perfectionism and High-Achieving Behaviors*
and *Living Beyond OCD Using Acceptance and Commitment Therapy*

"LeJeune's book stands out in bringing ACT to bear on the pure obsessions of OCD. With greater depth and clarity than others, he explains 'cognitive fusion' in this disorder, and develops the ideas of 'magic' and 'time fusion.' LeJeune shares pearls of wisdom in a highly engaging, readable, and practical manner."

—**Alan K. Louie, MD**, professor, associate chair, and director of education in the department of psychiatry and behavioral sciences at Stanford University School of Medicine

"With *'Pure O' OCD*, LeJeune has given us an expert guide through the twists and turns of the obsessive mind, illuminating the way with an engrossing blend of evidence-based strategy and story. Highly recommended for those hoping to revolutionize their relationship to intrusive thoughts, and by doing so, to break free."

—**Sheva Rajaee, MFT**, director of The Center for Anxiety and OCD, and author of *Relationship OCD*

"In *'Pure O' OCD*, Chad LeJeune tackles one of the most challenging forms of OCD. With his relatable and often humorous style, LeJeune offers a fresh and practical treatment guide by combining traditional exposure therapy with ACT. I have already added this book to my OCD toolbox, and will be encouraging many of my clients to do the same."

—**Scott M. Granet, LCSW**, author of *The Complete OCD Workbook*

"A truly excellent guide to coping with and recovering from an often neglected type of OCD. Packed full of useful information, essential skills, and empowering strategies, this is not only a really useful self-help book, but also an invaluable resource for any therapist who works with OCD. Highly recommended!"

—**Russ Harris**, author of the million-copy best-seller, *The Happiness Trap*

"A must-read for those suffering from obsessions—the 'sticky thoughts' that plague people with OCD. LeJeune provides a much-needed guide for getting 'unstuck' from thoughts that feel terrifying or disgusting. His decades of experience shine through every page as he brilliantly describes and illustrates how to disentangle from thoughts themselves, and choose values-based activities over mental or physical rituals. A life-transforming book for sufferers, and an invaluable clinical resource!"

—**Joan Davidson, PhD**, cofounder and codirector of the San Francisco Bay Area Center for Cognitive Therapy; and assistant clinical professor in the clinical science program at the University of California, Berkeley

For Melba K,
Warren,
and little Abby

Contents

"Pure O" and Sticky Thoughts

We all think, and we think all the time. Even in sleep, the wellspring of the mind brings forth a perpetual stream of thoughts. Images and reflections, hopes and regrets, fears and fancies, explanations and justifications, all are features of that vast internal landscape that is consciousness. Thoughts have allowed us to flourish as a species. They make it possible for us to anticipate and plan for the future, and to learn from the past. Thoughts allow us to solve complex problems, walking through limitless iterations without treading a single step. Thoughts provide a sense of orientation, not only to where we are, but to who we are. With their help, we organize and structure raw experience, weaving together the threads of our moments and narrating our journey.

Our thoughts are with us always, and though we trust and rely on them, our helpmeet can also oppress and deceive us. Our thoughts make it possible to anticipate and fear what does and does not wait in the future, and to regret and ruminate on that which lies in the past. They lead us along circuitous, treacherous paths, leaving us disoriented. In their thrall, we are robbed of raw experience and trapped in a web of narrative that limits our journey. This book is about how our thoughts become a source of suffering. In it, we will meet people who fear and struggle with their thoughts, exploring what causes and contributes to this struggle. Then, we will look at five skills that can help us to recognize and let go of this struggle, allowing us to live more fully in the moment and to move forward with a clearer sense of purpose.

The Jacket

Anthony didn't usually spend a lot of money on clothes, but he really liked this jacket. It was suede, and even though it had a nice, quilted lining, it wasn't too heavy or bulky. Sure, it was sort of expensive, but it was a jacket he could wear much of the year. It fit him well, too. It was the fact that he liked the jacket so much, as well as the expense, that made the sneezing incident so tragic.

It happened the second time he wore the jacket. He and Lisa had just finished a nice meal at a popular neighborhood restaurant. It was a Friday night, so the place was packed. As Anthony followed his girlfriend toward the door, they got stuck momentarily in a bottleneck of people. Because it was cold out, a crowd of people were waiting for tables just inside the door. The hostess was seating a large party and temporarily blocked Lisa's path. At the same time, an older gentleman and his wife were exiting right behind Anthony, and the guy ended up practically breathing down his neck. Of course, that's when it happened, the one moment when there was no escape. The old guy sneezed. Not once, but twice. There was no way to know if the guy was covering the sneezes. Anthony had more sense than to turn toward a sneezing person. He sort of felt the force of the sneezes on his back. He was wearing the jacket, so he couldn't literally feel it, but he sensed it. He also thought he might have felt a drop of something hit the exposed skin on the back of his neck. He was able to hold his breath long enough for the bottleneck to open up and for him and Lisa to make their way outside.

The first thing Anthony did once they were on the sidewalk was to get a look at the sneezer. He didn't want to be mean or ageist or anything, but the guy was kind of gross. What Anthony noticed most was that he had a sort of bulbous nose, with quite a bit of nose hair sticking out of it, and as he moved down the sidewalk, the guy was wiping his nose with a handkerchief. Anthony watched with growing disgust as the guy stuffed the rumpled handkerchief into his pocket. Clearly, these had been two wet sneezes. Anthony could wash his neck, but his thoughts were on the jacket.

Since he was just sort of standing there, Lisa asked a little anxiously, "What's wrong?" Anthony stepped closer to the curb and took a deep breath. He leaned in closer to Lisa, wincing slightly. He was careful to keep his voice low and controlled.

"That guy just sneezed all over me."

Lisa looked at him sympathetically and gave him a tight little smile. "Oh, honey…"

"Can you look at the back of my jacket and tell me if you see anything?"

They moved closer to a streetlight, and Lisa took a careful look. She said, "I don't see anything." She gave Anthony a reassuring pat on the arm. "I think it's fine."

"Are you sure? You don't see any little spots?" Despite the cold, Anthony carefully took off the jacket and gingerly held it up to the light. "What about there? What's that? Is that like a…droplet?"

Lisa did her best to reassure him, but for Anthony, the evening was ruined. When he got home, he put the jacket over a chair in the corner of his bedroom, quarantining it from the rest of his clothes. By now, the spot he thought he had seen earlier had evaporated, or whatever, but he knew it was there. After a few days he managed to move the jacket to his closet, but he hung it all the way to the left so that the back of it touched the wall and none of his other clothes. When he touched the jacket, all he could see was the bulbous nose and the nose hairs. He could see the wet handkerchief being stuffed in the guy's pocket, and a chill ran down his spine.

The following week, the weather turned colder, and there was a holiday party at work. It would have been nice to wear the jacket, but he couldn't bring himself to do it. For Anthony, the jacket was covered in old guy snot. He wondered if he could maybe have it dry cleaned or something, but he knew from experience that this would probably not make any difference. What was on that jacket, no amount of cleaning could remove. Like so many articles of clothing before it, this beautiful, expensive jacket was destined to spend months, maybe years, at the back of his closet. Eventually it would be cast out, banished to a consignment shop or even Goodwill. Such a shame. Anthony really liked that jacket.

The Sociopath

Sophie had always been very close to her parents. Maybe it was because she was an only child. Maybe it was because they were both just such cool parents. After college, she had moved back home for a year to save money while she looked for her first serious job, and she really liked living with them. She had plenty of friends and enjoyed going out, but she was also very happy to stay home and hang out with her mom and dad.

That's why, when she finally moved out into her own place, she was surprised that she didn't miss them more. Granted, she was living in the same city, and even on the same side of town as her parents, but she didn't see nearly as much of them as before. She really liked her job and had made some great new friends there. Between new friends and old friends, and dating more than she ever had before, she was pretty busy. She called her parents a few times a week, and got over to their house pretty much every weekend. They were even planning a vacation together. Still, she was surprised at how little she thought about them some weeks. As close as they had always been, she would have expected to feel sad and to miss them more.

When she was away at college, she had often felt homesick and anxious. She had spent a lot of time on the phone talking to both her mom and dad then. When she had moved back home, it felt natural to keep them posted on everything that was happening in her life. Now, for some reason, she seemed more distant from them. She wondered why. Was there something wrong with her? I mean, did she really even love her parents at all?

Whenever Sophie thought about this question, she got very uncomfortable. Sometimes she felt guilty, and tears sprang to her eyes. She tended to deal with this by immediately calling or texting her parents, no matter what time it was, just to tell them that she loved them. On the phone, when she said, "I love you guys," she could really get choked up. Yet when she hung up, she found herself thinking, "But do I really? How do I know that I love my parents? What if I just know that I'm supposed to feel that way, and so I convince myself that I do?" The idea that she couldn't know for sure if she really felt something or if she just imagined she felt it really freaked her out.

These thoughts often came to her at night, right after she got in bed and turned out the light. To reassure herself, she would sometimes think about her parents dying. She got into the habit of imagining either her mother or her father's funeral. Sometimes she would imagine that they had both been killed in an accident, and that it was a double funeral. She would imagine herself sitting in church, seeing her parents lying in their caskets, and think about the fact that she would never be able to talk to them again. When she thought about this, she felt kind of sad, and she didn't like the images at all. Yet, she thought, "If I really loved my parents, wouldn't the idea of them dying make me cry?" She tried to bring herself to tears with these images, but couldn't. She even tried listening to sad music while she imagined the double funeral of her parents. Nothing.

Then one night, Sophie had an image of herself standing calm and tearless over her parents' graves (this time she had imagined a graveside service). It was raining, and all of her relatives were standing around under black umbrellas, sobbing their eyes out. But Sophie was just looking at her phone. As upsetting as this image was, Sophie could not get it out of her mind. That's when it occurred to her what might be wrong. Maybe she was a sociopath! Sophie's heart raced at this thought, and she broke into a cold sweat. Again, tears sprang to her eyes, and she shook her head violently at the thought. "Oh, God, please...no! I don't want to be a sociopath!" Maybe it wasn't true. Maybe it was just a thought. It seemed like she had feelings about things, but again, what if she was just pretending. What if she was such a good sociopath that she had even fooled herself?! How could she know for sure?

Cat's in the Cradle

Lou had a good life. He was successful in his work, he loved his wife, and he had an eight-year-old son, Adam, who thought he walked on water. Lou wanted more than anything to be a good dad. He worked long hours during the week, but always found time to play a video game or read a book with Adam at bedtime. On the weekends, they often went to the beach together, just the two of them. They waded in the surf or built elaborate sand castles, talking about all sorts of things. Adam loved science and nature and wanted to be a marine biologist.

Lou felt so close to his son, and was so aware of how special this time together was, that he hated to think about Adam growing up. He could imagine that maybe by the time he was in his teens, he wouldn't want to hang out with his dad so much. This was a very painful thought for Lou, but once it had occurred to him, it was hard not to think about. It often popped into his head just when he was having a good time with Adam.

He would think about how Adam was likely to become more social once he hit middle school. Maybe he would even have a best friend. With buddies his own age to play video games and hang out with, Adam would inevitably pull away from Lou. Surely by high school, they wouldn't be as close as they are now. Some nights, driving home from work, Lou thought about this and cried a little. The worst was when he saw a commercial or a sappy TV program about some kid going away to college. You've seen it a hundred times: A leafy campus, parents unloading a station wagon, the kid awkwardly connecting with peers…then the tearful goodbye. Lou had to either change the channel or leave the room.

He tried to stop these painful thoughts, but they kept coming. After a while, it was like they were always there, at the edge of his mind, waiting to spring upon him. Since seeing Adam was a trigger for these thoughts, some nights he found himself lingering at the office, putting off going home. If he was feeling vulnerable to the thoughts on a given night, he sometimes cut things short at bedtime, skipping the book or video game, in spite of Adam's protests. There were fewer trips to the beach on weekends. The closeness he felt to his son when they played together in the sand only intensified the thoughts of them inevitably growing apart. Lou was heartsick and distraught. What had happened to his good life?

OCD and "Pure O"

Anthony, Sophie, and Lou—three of several composite figures you'll meet, modeled on patients I have worked with—are very different people with one thing in common. All of them are struggling to control thoughts that they find upsetting or disturbing. Paradoxically, their fear of these thoughts, and their efforts to avoid or control them, actually serves to keep the thoughts there, and to refresh them over and over again. This cycle of anxiety about thoughts leading to more anxiety-producing thoughts constitutes an *obsession.*

All three of our obsessing friends have learned to do things that give them temporary relief from the obsessions. Anthony avoids wearing the "contaminated" jacket, Sophie calls her parents to profess her love, and, most poignantly, Lou avoids spending time with his son. These efforts to escape from the anxiety of obsessive thoughts are called *compulsions.* They are moves that anxious people feel compelled to make to escape from anxiety. These moves can take the form of simple avoidance or of more complex behavioral or mental rituals. Unfortunately, the escape these moves provide is only temporary. What's more, the relief they provide reinforces the compulsion, making the avoidant or reassuring behaviors addictive in a certain way. When this pattern happens repeatedly, is distressing to the individual, and interferes with their daily life, we can say that the person is struggling with *obsessive-compulsive disorder* (OCD). This is simply a label used to describe a pattern of feelings (anxiety), thoughts (obsessions), and behaviors (compulsions) that appears often enough to be labeled and studied by behavioral scientists.

When we talk about OCD, most people think of contamination fears, or "germaphobia," and the compulsive washing and cleaning that often accompanies it. A related image is the person who engages in super-stitious rituals, like counting or ordering objects, to deal with their anxiety. A good example of this widely held picture of OCD is that depicted by Jack Nicholson in *As Good as It Gets*. This movie does a great job of showing one man's struggle with OCD and the costs of that strug-gle in terms of isolation and compromised values.

While this may be the most well-known image of a person with OCD, the fact is that it can take on an infinite variety of forms. Many people with OCD struggle with obsessions that have nothing at all to do with contamination or cleanliness, and engage in compulsions that are more subtle than washing or ordering objects. In many cases, the compulsions are literally invisible and take the form of avoidance or thought rituals intended to provide reassurance.

For example, while Anthony's anxiety about his sneezed-on jacket might seem to reveal a fear of germs, if we look more closely we can see that's not the case at all. The thoughts and images that Anthony is afraid of, and that have attached themselves to the jacket, are more about the sneezing itself, as well as the older gentleman's nose and his used handker-chief. What disturbs Anthony is not germs or a fear of getting sick, but rather the "ick" factor of the experience and the idea of "old guy snot" that the jacket now brings to mind. This is an example of what has been called *emotional contamination*. Anthony doesn't bother to have the jacket cleaned because he seems to know that the contamination is emotional, rather than microbial. Rather than cleaning, the compulsions in this case are the sequestering of the jacket from his other clothes and his avoidance of wearing it again. Avoidance can be subtle and harder to detect than an overt compulsion like washing or cleaning.

When a compulsion is thought-based, or cognitive, it is invisible. When Sophie's anxiety prompted her to call her parents and profess her love for them, this was an overt, observable ritual. Imagining their death and funeral, although covert and thought-based, was also a ritual. Like the calls to her parents, this cognitive ritual was an effort to get reassur-ance and relief from the obsessive fear that she did not *really* love her parents. She may not have thought of it as a ritual, and if she spoke to a therapist about it, they may not see it as such. Moreover, for Sophie and Lou, whose obsessive thoughts involve their feelings for loved ones, talking with a therapist about those feelings, examining them over and over again in detail, and getting reassurance about them can become a compulsive ritual in itself. This could lead to years of paying to "obsess out loud" to a well-intentioned therapist. Like any compulsion, the temporary relief of doing this makes the behavior addictive—while doing little to diminish the anxiety related to the obsessive thoughts when they inevitably return.

Because their obsessions don't fit the stereotype of germaphobia, or because their compulsions are invisible, many people struggling with OCD are misdiagnosed by therapists. Therapists trained in cognitive behavioral therapy or acceptance and commitment therapy—the basis of this book, which we'll discuss shortly—tend to be more familiar with the full range of forms that OCD can take. When a person has obsessions, but the compulsions or rituals of OCD are not readily apparent, some therapists use the unofficial term "Pure O" to emphasize that obsessions are the dominant symptom. In these cases, it is important to realize that compulsions are almost always present as well. Compulsions may include subtle avoidance of triggers, reassuring thought-based rituals, questioning of friends and family to gain reassurance, or even just "confessing" to the thoughts by talking about or around them with others. While all of these responses offer temporary relief in the short term, they are much more a part of the problem than a part of a solution. Because the uncertainty they are intended to address can never be completely eliminated, cognitive rituals tend to be repeated over and over again, often in increasingly elaborate ways. The time and energy devoted to these rituals can be a huge drain on personal resources that could be better applied to activities, relationships, and other pursuits that add value to life. Constantly requesting reassurance and confessing or discussing obsessive thoughts with others shifts this burden to loved ones and can take a serious toll on relationships. Finally, the persistent avoidance of people and pursuits that trigger obsessive thoughts can be the most insidious and costly compulsion of all.

Treatment of OCD

The past decade has seen a great deal of progress in the treatment of OCD, in particular through the use of exposure and response prevention (ERP). ERP emphasizes identifying even subtle or invisible compulsions and asking clients to intentionally engage their obsessions while blocking the compulsive avoidance or other relieving behaviors. Over time, this leads to diminishing anxiety and an "extinction" of the compulsive behavior. ERP is an effective treatment approach and is fully compatible with the ideas presented in this book. Because it emphasizes a change in behavior, it is often part of cognitive behavioral therapy for OCD, which also focuses on changing, or "restructuring," the distortions in thoughts caused by anxiety. Acceptance and commitment therapists also tend to make ERP a central part of their treatment for OCD, though they emphasize the development of a different set of skills that focus more on changing your relationship to distorted thoughts, rather than changing the thoughts themselves.

It makes sense that clinical research on OCD has focused on "response prevention." The compulsive, behavioral part of OCD is often the most obvious to an outside observer, and also the easiest to track and measure. Empirical studies require measurable outcomes to demonstrate a treatment's effectiveness. This is important and has led to more use of empirically supported treatments by therapists. This book, however, will focus more on the *thought* part of OCD, and the Pure O variety of OCD in particular. We will talk about compulsive behavior, including avoidance, mental rituals, reassurance seeking, and compulsive checking, but I believe that the key to getting relief from OCD lies not only in preventing compulsions, but in actually changing your relationship to obsessive thoughts. If you can learn to struggle less with your thoughts, you will obsess less. Less obsessing leads to fewer compulsions. The other element emphasized here, which is often missing in treatment focused solely on ERP, is what to do instead of compulsive behaviors. If my choices are not driven by my anxiety and obsessions, how will I decide what to do or how to act? An important part of our discussion will be about identifying and acting on your *values*. When we focus on what we value and on translating that into action, we are often moved to act in ways that run counter to compulsive behaviors. To the extent that this book addresses compulsions, it is less about "Stop that," and more about "What is the value of doing that?"

Changing the *relationship* between your *self* and your thoughts and increasing an awareness of and *commitment* to acting on your *values* are the key components of acceptance and commitment therapy (ACT). This therapy model, developed by psychologist Steven C. Hayes and his colleagues over the past thirty years, has been proven to be effective in the treatment of a broad range of emotional and behavioral problems. ACT captured my imagination early in my clinical career and has shaped my understanding of more than just OCD. I trained with Dr. Hayes in the early 1990s, when the ACT approach was in its infancy (it wasn't even called ACT back then). Aside from being a treatment model, ACT is sort of a way of thinking about thoughts. It helps us look more closely at how we experience the world, asking questions like

"How do thoughts relate to reality?"

"What is the difference between you and your experience?"

"How do we decide what to do at a given moment?"

It takes a little patience to examine questions like this, but they happen to be just the right questions for a person struggling with OCD to ask.

A central concept of ACT is something called *cognitive fusion.* If you continue to read this book, you'll become very familiar with this term. *Cognitive fusion* refers to the failure of the anxious part of the brain to make a clear distinction between a thought and the reality that the thought refers to (its *referent*). In other words, the thought becomes more *sticky,* "fusing" with the corresponding reality in our experience of it. When this happens, we experience the *idea* of, for example, "old guy snot" (the thought) and *actual* old guy snot (the referent) as the same thing. Or we experience the idea that we might not love our parents as an actual lack of love. Or the mere possibility of alienation from a beloved child— which, like all possibilities, exists solely as a thought—crushes us with the weight of actual loss. Intellectually, we may be quite clear that these thoughts are not the same thing as the reality they reference, but on an *experiential* level, they are the same. This is cognitive fusion. The sticky thoughts it produces are the main subject of this book.

Cognitive fusion can cause us to become *afraid* of our thoughts. This is essentially a description of OCD, and why I think ACT is so well suited for addressing all forms of OCD, especially Pure O. When we struggle to control or avoid certain thoughts, it's because cognitive fusion has led the mind to perceive these thoughts as a threat. Understanding and interrupting this phenomenon is key to shifting the relationship between you and your obsessive thoughts.

About This Book

Part one of this book is all about sticky thoughts. Why thoughts become sticky, how it happens, and the implications of it happening not just for obsessions, but for all forms of struggle with our thoughts. More fully understanding the concept of cognitive fusion can help you to identify it when it's happening, label it, and observe it. This creates the space between *you* and your *experience* necessary for shifting your relationship to your thoughts and letting go of your struggle with them. This space also creates the opportunity for the opposite of cognitive fusion: *cognitive de-fusion.* This is when thoughts become more *separate* from their referents, or less sticky. When this happens, we experience the idea of "snot" or "contamination" as separate and distinct from actual snot or contamination, and completely separate from the jacket (you may *think* it's snot... but it's...not).

Part two is all about making thoughts less sticky by creating defusion. This section introduces five skills, or steps, toward getting thoughts and yourself unstuck: *Labeling* fused thoughts; *Letting go* of the struggle to control thoughts; *Accepting* thoughts as thoughts; being *Mindful* of the present moment; and acting with a sense of *Purpose,* guided by your values instead of by anxiety or compulsions. These five skills are captured in the acronym LLAMP. Chapters six through ten introduce each of the skills individually along with specific tools and exercises to help you develop that skill. The final chapter of the book is about using the five skills together to tilt away from cognitive fusion, struggle, and acting compulsively out of fear and toward being present and acting on your values. This could mean something as simple as wearing a jacket on a cold day, or something as complex as making a career change. It could mean pursuing old interests, or developing new skills. It may involve taking more risks, or spending more quality time with your family. Chances are, it will also mean less time battling your own thoughts, washing your hands, or straightening the rug.

PART ONE

How Thoughts Get Sticky

CHAPTER 1

The Thing in the Bushes

We tend to think of anxiety as a problem to be solved. As a therapist who specializes in *treating* anxiety, I have to acknowledge that my very existence supports this paradigm. New patients call my office because they "have anxiety." The clear implication is that anxiety, in and of itself, is a problem. One of the first things I try to point out to any new patient is that we all have anxiety. Not only human beings, but all animals, are hardwired for anxiety. Not only that, far from being a problem, per se, anxiety is crucial for our survival as individuals, and as a species. Sometimes this goes over well. Other times, the response is something like "Well, yeah…but you know what I mean." Let me just start by saying, here, in chapter one…that I do, indeed. Anxiety can be present more often, and at higher levels, than we like. Our struggles to reduce anxiety can escalate it, and our efforts to mitigate or avoid it can lead to any number of very serious problems. Still, it is important to begin with the fact that we all have, and always will have, anxiety. Saying "I have anxiety" is somewhat like saying "My heart is beating" or "I'm breathing a lot" (which are, incidentally, two things that I also hear from many new patients).

A Brief History of Fear

The story of anxiety starts with the thing in the bushes. For most of our time on this planet, we were surrounded by bushes…or trees, or boulders. The problem with these otherwise innocuous landscape features was that they provided cover for other, larger animals that could easily damage our soft, permeable bodies. Over millennia, those bodies developed a complex system for anticipating, preparing for, and responding to this and other threats to our well-being. This is our famous, ancient *fight-or-flight response.* It is key to both our survival and our struggles. It contributes to our success, as well as to our suffering.

So...you're walking through the forest, minding your own business, when suddenly you become aware of *something* coming toward you, through the bushes. You see and hear the bushes moving, but you do not yet know the cause of the movement. This is the beginning of anxiety. Anxiety is not so much the lion, tiger, or bear that's chasing you. That's not anxiety, that's a lion, tiger, or bear. And when you're being chased, you're not exactly anxious. You're running. Anxiety is what happens just before you're being chased. It's also what happens before you're *not* being chased. *That* is the problem.

Anxiety is what prepares you to run, or to stand and fight for your life. The problem is, this happens whether the thing in the bushes is a lion, tiger, or bear or a cute little bunny rabbit that just wants to be your friend. If there are a lot of bunnies around, you are going to be anxious a lot of the time. Also, if you're a fast enough runner, you might not meet any of them, much less get to be friends. Anxiety is the response that protects you from threats, as well as from opportunities. The reason is that both of these are in the bushes. Just understanding more about how the fight-or-flight response works can help us choose how we respond to it. I like to break it down into changes below the neck and changes above the neck.

Fight-or-Flight Below the Neck

Mechanically speaking, the primary objective of fight-or-flight is to get as much blood as possible into the large muscles of your back, arms, and legs. These are the muscles involved in fighting and flying. To accomplish this, the heart starts beating faster, and blood pressure rises (which can make us feel hot and uncomfortable). More blood leads to more tension in these muscles (which can lead to trembling as well as muscle aches and pain). We start to breathe more, and higher in our chest, to bring more oxygen to these muscles (which can eventually leave us light-headed or dizzy). The flow of blood away from the small muscles in our scalp, hands, and feet has the added benefit of making us less likely to bleed out if we're bitten or scratched in these vulnerable areas (but it can also lead to weird tingling in the scalp, hands, or feet). We might start to perspire, both to cool off and to make our bodies more slippery and harder to catch (this can also make a mess of our clothes, if we're wearing any). Finally, since the last thing you want to do if an animal is stalking you is stop to poop, our digestive tract shuts down, from top to bottom (which means dry mouth and "butterflies" in the stomach).

Once all of these changes have kicked in, you're good to go. You are physically ready to run much faster and fight back much harder than you were before fight-or-flight kicked in. Unfortunately, you are also a bit of a mess. All these physical changes bring a degree of discomfort, which can, in itself, be a trigger for more anxiety. If the thing in the bushes is indeed a lion, tiger, or bear, this is not a problem. In this primal scenario, the fight-or-flight response, while intense, is also fairly short-lived. It lasts just long enough for you to fend of the attacking predator and run to safety, or…not. In the better primal scenario, once you've scrambled to the top of the tree and can see that you are safe, all systems slowly return to normal. Most of us call this *relief*. Biologists call it a *parasympathetic response,* which is the opposite of the fight-or-flight response. It involves things like sighing, crying, laughing, and eventually yawning and sleep. All of this helps our body return to baseline.

However, since fight-or-flight kicks in not only when we're about to be chased but also when we *think* we're about to be chased, it's possible for us to find ourselves in this heightened state much of the time. This chronic overarousal can lead to things like muscle pain, headaches, high blood pressure, indigestion, irritable bowels, and countless other ailments. If we take a closer look at what's happening, we see that fight-or-flight is often not so much a response to a lion, tiger, or bear as a response to the *thought* "Oh shit! It's a lion, tiger, or bear!" or even the *thought "What if eventually* it's a lion, tiger, or bear?"

Technically, it's a bit more complicated. Sensory information goes directly to the amygdala, which is the fight-or-flight center of the brain.

The amygdala can respond to this input directly, without what we usually think of as *thought*. This is why we can have a startle response to an object flying toward us before we process what it is. However, the amygdala can also respond to thoughts and stories generated by the more sophisticated, thinking part of the brain (the cortex). This is what happens when we suddenly realize that something has gone wrong, when we imagine that something may go wrong in the future, or even when we remember something that went very wrong in the past. When it comes to OCD, the amygdala can learn to respond to something as simple as a word or an image with the full fight-or-flight response.

Whether or not, and to what degree, fight-or-flight is triggered by our thoughts depends on two things:

1. the *content* of our thoughts, and

2. our *relationship* to that content.

This brings us to what I like to think of as fight-or-flight above the neck.

Fight-or-Flight Above the Neck

Fight-or-flight affects the functioning of our brains. It causes a shift in how we perceive the world, the thoughts we have about those perceptions, and our relationship to those thoughts. When something is coming through the bushes, we become *hypervigilant*. In other words, we are more aware of certain sensory information that could be relevant to the threat. Our hearing becomes sharper, but only for certain, threat-related sounds. Our vision becomes more focused, but only on the area directly in front of us. In fact, we lose a certain amount of peripheral vision. All of this contributes to what we call a *threat bias*, or a tendency to perceive things as more threatening than they actually are. This threat bias applies not only to what we notice and attend to in the environment, but to what conclusions we draw from that information.

Threat bias affects the *content* of our thoughts, in that we are more likely to interpret otherwise neutral information as threatening. This is because, in the thing-in-the-bushes scenario, there is survival value in assuming that there is a threat. This means you are more likely to run away. This was adaptive and helpful when we were surrounded by predator-filled bushes. In the primeval forest, it paid to err on the side of caution. In the modern world, this is not always the case. Often, anxiety can cause us to run away from rewards and opportunities as well as threats. In fact, the modern world often rewards a certain amount of risk taking. Think about applying for a better job, investing in the stock market, or asking someone out on a date.

It's not just the *content* of our thoughts that changes as part of fight-or-flight. There is also a *contextual* or *relational* shift in the way we experience our thoughts. When we're anxious, we often experience our thoughts as more than just thoughts. In other words, we respond to the *thought* of a lion, tiger, or bear the same way we would respond to an *actual* lion, tiger, or bear. This is cognitive fusion. It means that the *thought* of a lion coming through the bushes, and an a*ctual* lion coming through the bushes, are *fused* in our experience. The amygdala and the body respond to the *thoughts* the same way they would respond to the *reality* that the thoughts refer to. This leads to more anxiety and more running, whether there is a lion or not.

Like the fight-or-flight response, both threat bias and cognitive fusion developed in our species because they had survival value. The person without threat bias (what we might now call an optimist) always assumed that the thing in the bushes was a cute little bunny rabbit looking to make a new friend. While this sort of thinking may have initially contributed to a wide circle of bunny friends, it eventually resulted in a tasty, optimist-flavored lunch for a lucky lion, tiger, or bear. The same is true for the enlightened primeval individual who was mindfully and insightfully aware of their thoughts. Just *noticing* the arising thought of a lion or tiger, but waiting for more information, may work 99% of the time. Eventually, though…another lunch, this time the mindful special. There is ultimately survival value in running in response to the thought of the lion, tiger, or bear…even if 99% of the time it's only a bunny. In the long run, it was the non-optimistic, non-insightful, frightened individuals who were constantly running from bunnies who survived to pass their genes along to us. Thanks to our anxious ancestors, we are not only pessimists, we are masters of cognitive fusion. The more anxious we become, the more likely we are not only to expect negative outcomes, but to respond to our *thoughts* about those outcomes the same way we would respond to the *reality* the thoughts refer to.

Language and Suffering

While the fight-or-flight response is something we hold in common with other animals, cognitive fusion appears to be unique to humans. Before we can have cognitive fusion, we must have cognition. Human-style thinking is part and parcel of our unique capacity for language. Whether in the form of words, concepts, or images, *thoughts* can be understood as internal language. Like spoken or written words, thoughts are symbolic, analog representations of the external world. Thought, like language, is a map that refers to a territory that lies elsewhere. Cognitive fusion is an instance of what semantics scholar Alfred Korzybski (1933) referred to as mistaking the "map for the territory." He put it even more succinctly when he said, "The word is not the thing."

Our capacity for language has allowed us to solve very complex problems, plan ahead, and share our complicated ideas with one another. It has also made us the only animal that can be safe, dry, rested, and well fed, and still be completely miserable. This is because language allows *judgment*. Before language, we simply had an experience. After language, we could compare that experience to other experiences, even imaginary experiences, and find it lacking. We can also judge the past and the future. Language affords us the ability to have not only a bad moment, but also a bad day, a terrible year, or an unfortunate life. Language (and thinking) is both a blessing and a curse. It's not just judgment, it's also things like memory and anticipation. Even when we are having what we judge to be a "good" experience, we can easily revisit pain from the past or anticipate our nice experience turning into something shitty. This is not a new idea. Human beings have been aware of the mixed blessing of language for a very long time.

Adam and Eve and Steve

As a student therapist, I was initially exposed to ACT at a series of weekend retreats that Steve Hayes hosted in his home. I remember these weekends as intellectually exciting, emotionally intense, and extremely fun. They included collaborative meals, sing-alongs, and graduate students in sleeping bags all over the floor. A small detail that stayed with me from my very first retreat was a framed woodcut hanging on the wall in Steve's living room. It was a depiction of the story of Adam and Eve: simple, folk art images of Adam, Eve, the serpent, and the tree. It made an impression because it seemed somehow incongruent with the setting and the event. Coming from a background of Sunday School and Bible Camp, I saw this as a story about authority and obedience, arbitrary rules, and somewhat disproportionate punishment. It was not until some time later that I heard Steve's more behavioral and linguistic understanding of this primal story of the very beginnings of human experience (Hayes, Strosahl, and Wilson 1999).

As you may recall, Adam and Eve were quite content in their garden, the original paradise. They existed in perfect harmony with their environment, and with the other animals. Like them, they were naked and free of shame or judgment. Then they ate some bad fruit. Suddenly, things did not look so great. Adam and Eve looked around and got all judgy. They noticed that they were naked and felt ashamed. Things went downhill from there. Paradise was lost.

For Steve, the key to understanding the story lies in the exact name of the tree that produced the forbidden fruit. In case you haven't read the original in a while, it was "the tree of the knowledge of good and evil." In other words, the tree with the fruit that allows us to evaluate things as either nice or shitty. From a linguistic, semantic, psychological perspective, this is a story about what happened when human beings developed the capacity for judgmental, evaluative language and thought. It represents our "fall" from a nonjudgmental, in-the-moment harmony with our experience to the judgmental, regretting-and-anticipating, discordant struggle that we know so well. For me, this was a completely different way to understand this story, and one that had so many implications for how we operate as humans. It's a psycholinguistic reading of Genesis, or, as I like to think of it, the Story of Adam and Eve, and Steve.

Experiencing Thoughts as Thoughts

While Adam and Eve are central figures in Western culture, Eastern traditions also describe a connection between judgment, or evaluative thoughts, and suffering. Buddhist teaching warns of the pitfalls of attachment to our own thoughts and ideas. Buddhist meditation practices emphasize separating ourselves from the content of consciousness through mindful observation and regarding thoughts as thoughts, rather than the reality they refer to. Other practices, like chanting, attempt to directly break down the hold of language and thought over our experience. The same can be said of mystical or ecstatic rituals that focus the senses on the present moment, allowing us to detach from our thoughts. Think burning incense, reverberating gongs, or whirling dervishes. All of these practices create an environment in which experience is primary, independent of a verbal narrative.

Spiritual traditions do not hold a monopoly on this idea of getting distance from our own thinking. Engrossing activities like knitting, cooking, or fly fishing require us to be more focused and aware of the present moment. When this happens, the internal narrative of our thoughts has less of a hold on us. The same thing happens for many people when they go for a walk. While it's possible to walk for miles and remain engrossed in your thoughts, many walkers find that engagement with the natural world or the animation of an urban environment "clears the head" and offers a different perspective on their thoughts. Other people accomplish the same thing by listening to music, petting a cat or dog, or relaxing in a warm bath. This shift in our relationship to our inner narrative is very similar to the move toward cognitive defusion referred to in the introduction.

Struggling: The Gorilla in the Room

We have thoughts all day long. They show up like friends, neighbors, or delivery people arriving at our front door. They arrive with the morning sun, saying things like *Time to get up, Coffee!* and *What am I doing today?* We tend to listen to and follow most of these thoughts without question. They are our friends. Usually, we are so in harmony with our thoughts that we hardly notice them at all.

When anxious thoughts show up, however, it can be a little like getting a surprise visit from a gorilla. We often don't expect it, when, "ding-dong," we open the door and see a big, hairy, 400-pound gorilla standing on the welcome mat. Before we know it, he's in the room with us, and the door has closed behind him! Nobody likes anxiety. Like having a gorilla in the room, it's very uncomfortable. It's supposed to be. It's the function of anxiety to get our attention and to hold it…to get us to do something. When faced with an out-of-control situation, we try to either escape it or control it. If there's a fire in the building, we either leave the building or try to put the fire out. Since this gorilla is anxiety, and the anxiety is inside of us, escape is not really an option. Instead, we tend to try to control or contain this uncomfortable, seemingly dangerous thing. This amounts to grabbing the gorilla and doing our best to move him toward the door.

I don't know if this has ever happened to you, but in my experience, gorillas tend to resist this sort of redirection. If you grab onto a 400-pound gorilla, the next thing you know, you're likely to be rolling around on the floor wrestling with a 400-pound gorilla. Arguably, this is worse than just having it in the room. In fact, the harder you fight to get the gorilla out of the room, the more the gorilla fights back…and the more likely it is to stay in the room. There is paradox folded into our efforts to control both thoughts and anxiety. Because of this paradox, what starts out as a 400-pound gorilla can quickly become a 500-pound gorilla…and then a 600-pound gorilla. You get the idea. Most of us know intuitively that the harder we try to get rid of a thought, the more insistently the thought is just there. One paradox is that it's impossible to think about getting rid of a thought without thinking about that thought. Once we are struggling to keep a thought out of our consciousness, that thought has already breached the wall. Struggling with it only makes the thought more central to our experience. There's a similar paradox at work when we struggle to control the anxiety itself.

Control Is the Problem

The more we try to control our anxiety, the more anxious we feel. It pushes against the lid we try to put on it. The reason for this paradox is surprisingly simple. The one thing that your brain and body give you to help you control anything is...anxiety. Arousal, activation, energy, fight-or-flight. Call it what you will, control and anxiety are pretty much the same thing. Whether it's the slight increase in your heart rate that pushes you to do something about the coffee you just spilled on your friend's new sofa, or the full-throttle activation that helps you to extinguish the grease fire in your kitchen, this escalation of anxiety accompanies our efforts to control anything, even if that thing is anxiety itself. The gorilla stays even though you struggle to make it go because the gorilla is *made* of struggling. The reason it gets bigger and stronger the harder you try to control it is because this gorilla is *made* of control. Struggling and control, which seem to be part of the solution, are actually much of the problem.

Trying to control anxiety and get rid of anxious thoughts is like trying to clean up a little spilled water with more water. *Oops, I dribbled on the linoleum. Let me pour a little water on that. Darn, now I have a puddle. Let me get a bucket of water and rinse that away. Holy cow! What a mess. I'll have to hose this down... Good Lord! It's a flood! Call the Fire Department!*

Most obsessions start out as just thoughts. Granted, they are usually unpleasant thoughts. We have unpleasant thoughts all the time without necessarily trying to change or get rid of them. We have thoughts about unpleasant developments: *It's going to rain, and I don't have an umbrella.* We have unpleasant judgments: *This music sucks!* These thoughts aren't obsessions, though, because we are willing to have them. Good or bad, thoughts come and go all day long. There's sort of a *flow* to thoughts. When we decide we shouldn't have a particular thought, and make an effort to banish, change, or otherwise control that thought, this flow is interrupted. Like the gorilla, the thought we grab hold of tends to stick around. An obsession is simply a thought that you're not willing to have. If you're not resisting the thought, if you choose not to struggle with it, if you are *willing* to have it...it's just a thought.

It's About the Relationship

Like any struggle, the struggle between you and your thoughts is a relational problem. You have relationships with other people in your life, some of which are more harmonious, and others that are complicated by elements of struggle: judgment, avoidance, conflict. Most relationships involve a mixture of sympathy and strife. What's true for your relationships with people applies to other aspects of your life as well. For example, think about your relationship with your job or career, with your role as a parent or as a child. What about your relationship with your body or your relationship with food? Obsessing and the struggle it involves has everything to do with the relationship between you and your thoughts. Or if you prefer, your relationship with the gorilla in the room.

The most fundamental thing about a relationship is that it involves two entities. Before you can work on your relationship with your thoughts, it's essential to make a distinction between the two entities: (1) *you* and (2) your *thoughts*. Because we experience our thoughts as happening inside our heads, which is the same place we ourselves reside, we tend not to make a clear distinction between our *selves* and our thoughts. If we *are* our thoughts, then there's no relationship; it's all us. When this is our perception, the tendency is to accept whatever our mind offers us. When the thought is something like *It's cold out, I should wear my new jacket,* this isn't really a problem. My agenda of keeping warm and looking nice are in alignment with those thoughts. However, if it's cold out and my anxious mind says, *Unfortunately, that jacket is permanently contaminated with old guy snot,* it helps to see that there are two entities, each with a different agenda. While I want to be warm and look nice, my anxious mind wants to protect me from thinking about mucus. All too often, we lose sight of this distinction. It's as though the anxious mind says, *I am you. My agenda is your agenda.* When this happens, we can find ourselves fully aligned with the OCD and fighting alongside it as an ally. We actually find ourselves saying things like *I don't want to wear that jacket,* which we know to be categorically false. It turns out, the agenda we're fighting against is our own. In service of our fear, and the obsessive thoughts, we move further away from the things we value most. This eventually leaves us standing out in the cold...with no jacket.

With all of this talk about two entities, it's important to emphasize that we're not talking about two selves, or even about two parts of yourself. Your self is the you that has been there all your life, watching, listening, experiencing—the enduring *context* of all that you experience. Thoughts, on the other hand, are just another part of your experience. They're *content.* You experience what you see; what you hear; things you touch, taste, and smell. You experience emotions, and you experience thoughts. The two entities in all of these cases are *you* (your *self*) and your *experience.* You are the observer, and the experience is whatever you observe. The most fundamental relationship is between your *self* and your *experience.* The problem with obsessive thoughts is that this relationship is characterized by a struggle for control.

CHAPTER 2

Stickiness and Suffering

As fear increases, so does cognitive fusion, increasing the chances that we will respond to anxious thoughts with more anxiety or avoidance. In the last chapter, we looked at why this is the case. The increased stickiness of our thoughts gives us an evolutionary edge in dangerous situations. When our response to those thoughts helps us to deal more effectively with immediate threats, or even to anticipate and avoid future threats, a certain amount of stickiness can actually work in our favor. Often, though, buying into anxious thoughts is more problematic than helpful. In this chapter, we will examine the role that cognitive fusion plays in OCD in general, and in some of the most common patterns of Pure O. First, however, it may help to consider how fusion, or sticky thoughts, contributes to other, more straightforward anxiety-related problems.

Cognitive Fusion and Fear

Each of the problems we'll discuss in this chapter can be broken down into three components: anxiety, avoidance or control, and thoughts. We've covered anxiety pretty well. Avoidance or control strategies can include things like procrastination, overwork, or substance abuse. In OCD they often include compulsive behaviors like checking, performing rituals, and seeking reassurance. It's the third component of these problems that we are most concerned with here: thoughts. In all the problems we'll discuss below, sticky, fused thoughts play a central role. Each of these three components both feed into and are influenced by the other two components. For example, while more cognitive fusion (i.e., the thought component) leads to more anxiety, more anxiety causes our thoughts to be more fused. While anxiety leads to more avoidance, the more we avoid something, the more intensely we fear it. And while more cognitive fusion often means more avoidance, struggles to avoid certain thoughts often make those thoughts stickier. To see how this works, we'll start by looking at the role cognitive fusion plays in problems like phobias, social anxiety, and worry.

Phobias

Perhaps the most straightforward and easy to understand problematic fear is a phobia. This is an excessive, unreasonable fear of specific things or situations. Common phobias include fear of certain animals like spiders or snakes, fear of flying, and fear of heights. The thing to notice about phobias is that people who have them experience fear even when they are not actually around actual spiders or snakes, flying, or in a high place. When you talk to someone about their phobia, it becomes clear that their fear is largely a response to their specific *thoughts* about the things or situations that they fear. Often these thoughts take the form of a *narrative,* or story that supports the phobia. For many people with phobias, the narrative is as simple as "I'm afraid of _____." They may have learned this narrative at an early age. Consider the mother who notices that her two-year-old son is hesitant and fearful around dogs. Encountering someone with a dog on the street, she might pick the child up and say, "Timmy is afraid of dogs." Through cognitive fusion, this narrative can become a sort of verbal rule that Timmy learns and follows. At other times, the narrative may be a more detailed, often inaccurate or distorted story about the feared object or situation. Narratives like "Dogs often bite people" or "Airplanes often crash" become sticky and continue to produce anxiety even when shown to be false. The stickiness of these thoughts allows the phobic person to experience fear in the absence of the actual object or situation that the thoughts refer to. This, in turn, leads them to avoid those things. The avoidance prevents them from having experiences that might challenge or change those thoughts or narratives, thus maintaining the phobia.

Fear of flying is a good example. Over the past three decades, I have treated numerous patients presenting with a "fear of flying." A few simple questions usually reveal that, in almost every case, the individual seeking help is not, in fact, afraid of flying. In almost all of these cases, what they are actually afraid of is *crashing*. Yet in all this time, I have not met a patient who has experienced even a minor plane crash. In every case, their experience with crashing has been limited to *thoughts* about crashing. Now, we can all have thoughts about a plane crashing, and, on very turbulent flights, many of us do. For most of us, these are unpleasant thoughts about an outcome that we see as very bad, but unlikely. Because of cognitive fusion, the person with a phobia responds to the *thought* of crashing much the same way they would respond to *actually* crashing. First, since the anxious part of the brain does not make a clear distinction between the thought of crashing and actual crashing, they have a stronger fight-or-flight response. Second, they often avoid these thoughts by avoiding airplanes. Whereas crashing while flying is unlikely, thoughts of crashing are much more likely. For this reason, treatment plans for flying phobias often include sitting and practicing having detailed thoughts about crashing. Later, patients may even practice having these same thoughts while sitting on an airplane. Being able to fly means being willing to have thoughts of crashing. This is not the same thing as being willing to crash.

Something similar happens to the person with a spider phobia. Again, no spider is required. If they are in an environment where they even think a spider might be present, they respond to the thought of the spider with heightened anxiety and hypervigilance. The heightened sensory awareness can lead them to actually "feel" a spider crawling on their skin, resulting in even more anxiety, and sometimes even panic. Just as with flying and thoughts of crashing, it may not be unusual in certain settings, like an attic or crawl space, to have thoughts of spiders. It's when we experience these thoughts as *fused* with the experience of actual spiders that we have a problem. When our anxiety goes up at the very idea of a spider, we are much more likely to avoid attics or crawl spaces. This can reinforce a narrative like "Those places are full of spiders," which, because of our avoidance, is impossible to disprove.

Thoughts of negative outcomes are an unavoidable and even important part of situations where caution increases our safety. Let's say you are visiting an apartment on the twentieth floor of a high-rise. If you step out on the balcony for some fresh air, it's actually a good idea to remember that you are several stories above the ground. Because of this awareness, while you might approach the railing and even lean over it, you would probably not hop up and sit on the railing. If you paid close attention, you might even notice thoughts or images related to falling, or even jumping, coming to mind. This is your brain's way of saying, "Don't fall" or "Don't jump." While we may not like them, these are without a doubt helpful thoughts. For the person with a heights phobia, however, the stickiness of these thoughts can lead to sensations of actually falling. Sometimes the thoughts are mistaken for an "impulse" to jump. The fear, in both cases, is not of the high place so much as of the thoughts that it elicits.

Phobic Narratives in Pure O

When fears become focused more specifically on the thought part of our experience, they can qualify as obsessions. Remember the story of Anthony's snotty jacket from the introduction? Most of us would not diagnose Anthony with a jacket phobia. Would we say that he has a snot phobia? Not necessarily. Perhaps an old-guy-snot phobia? When we look closely at Anthony's avoidance of wearing the jacket, it's significant that he knows there is no snot on it. The problem is not snot, it's the *idea of contamination* itself. Anthony's anxiety is a response to the narrative of the old guy, his snot, and the jacket. While cognitive fusion plays a role in all problematic fears, with Pure O, it's pretty much the main event. The anxiety is explicitly a response to the thought. The avoidance or rituals are explicitly about getting rid of the thought. This is why Anthony doesn't bother to have the jacket cleaned. He knows the narrative will still be associated with the jacket, and this is what he wants to avoid. He is afraid of his own sticky thoughts. This is what makes it "Pure O" OCD rather than a phobia.

Sophie's anxiety is also a response to a narrative. Her story is "If I don't feel constant love for my parents, I may be a sociopath." Compulsively calling her parents and professing her love to them and her cognitive ritual of imagining their funerals are efforts to temporarily dispel that narrative. If she can conjure some feeling of love for her parents, it provides some reassurance that the narrative is not true. This can offer a temporary escape from her anxiety. Because the goal is reassurance, these types of rituals are often referred to as *reassurance seeking.*

Lou's Pure O is also a response to a narrative. For Lou, it's the story that his son will eventually grow distant from him and that they will lose the special bond they currently share. Lou's response is different from Sophie's. Instead of seeking reassurance, he begins to avoid spending time with his son in order to avoid triggering the narrative. This is more like Anthony's avoidance of the jacket. Lou does not have a "son phobia." He's afraid of the thoughts that come up when he's with his son. It's the fear of his thoughts that makes it OCD. It's the subtle, less obvious nature of his response that makes it Pure O.

Social Anxiety

Cognitive fusion is not so much about believing that our thoughts are true or real. On a rational level, we may doubt the truth or accuracy of our thoughts, or even believe that they're unlikely. We often know that these are "just thoughts." The problem is that we *experience* them as more than that. An example of this phenomenon that most of us can relate to is what happens when we experience anxiety about social situations. Imagine attending a networking event with a group that you are new to, but hope to impress. While some people look forward to this sort of thing, many of us feel at least a moderate prick of increased vigilance going in.

Because human beings are pack animals, there is survival value in being an accepted member of the group we are associating with. Evolutionarily speaking, individuals who were rejected by the group were more likely to die when they lost access to shared water and food resources. Being kicked out of the club also meant losing your gene pool privileges. As a result, over time, we developed brain functions that closely monitor cues in social interactions for any signs of negative evaluation or possible rejection, and respond to them as though they are life-threatening. Fight-or-flight kicks in, as outlined in the last chapter. Our blood pressure spikes, making us warmer, and perhaps causing us to blush. Our muscles tighten, making our movements stiff and clumsy, and perhaps making our hands or legs shake. We may even start to perspire. While none of these responses do a lot to improve our poise and ease in these situations, if members of the group do attack us physically, at least the sweat will make us more slippery and harder to catch.

More relevant to our discussion is what happens to our thoughts. Our increased anxiety creates a threat bias, leading us to assume the worst when reading social cues that are ambiguous. If we have trouble reading someone's response to us, we are more likely to have thoughts like *He doesn't like me* or *She thinks I'm boring*. It's not just the content of these thoughts that changes with anxiety, however; it's also our relationship to the thoughts. Our experience is not that the person *seems* to think we are lame. We *know* they think this. Anxiety in social situations gives us the temporary experience of being able to read other people's thoughts! Cognitive fusion leads us to experience these judgments not as our own thoughts but as the thoughts that other people are having...about us. This leads to more anxiety, which leads to more negative thoughts, and more cognitive fusion.

Not Being Good Enough

A related example of cognitive fusion that many of us have experienced is when we respond to new or challenging situations with an overly critical assessment of our worth or abilities. Since the anxious part of the brain wants to protect us from failure or falling short in some way, it can respond to these situations with fight-or-flight and the impulse to escape or avoid. While failure is always a *possibility* when we take on a new or difficult task, thanks to cognitive fusion, we can experience the narrative that we are incompetent or not good enough as unquestionably true. This leads some people to avoid trying new things. For others, it makes it difficult to accurately assess their performance. Even when we are presented with indicators of success or positive feedback, because of fusion, we can still *feel* like a failure or an imposter. I have met countless people over the years who, in spite of decades of success and achievement, cannot shake the sense that they are only fooling everyone, and that failure is imminent.

Worry

When our thoughts are negative, it can seem like they are just there to torment us and beat us down, discouraging us from traveling, meeting new people, and trying new things. In fact, our thoughts also point us in the direction of potential rewards and desirable outcomes. Thinking allows us to solve complex problems in the present, come to peace with the past, and even access hope about the future. Thinking changes, however, with the fight-or-flight response. Thoughts are not evolution's version of Netflix. They evolved to promote our survival, not to entertain us. They are blunt, imprecise instruments that err on the side of caution and become even more imprecise as anxiety increases. Because survival is their primary function, as perceived danger increases, thoughts will lean increasingly toward avoiding risk. *Worry* is the mind's attempt to predict future threats and possible negative outcomes. These thoughts usually take the form of "What if…"

Thinking about what may go wrong in the future can help us to plan or prepare. The problem is, when we are anxious, these thoughts can be a little like the meteorologist who, just to play it safe, predicts rain all day, every day, for the entire year: "Get your umbrellas out folks, and keep them out. In fact, keep them open. The forecast is rain, rain, and then more rain." To better protect us, the anxious brain overestimates the likelihood of negative events and outcomes. When we experience these thoughts in a fused way, our body can respond as though these negative events are happening now. Worry involves both excessive thoughts about negative outcomes and an accompanying physical arousal in response to those thoughts. Like carrying an open umbrella everywhere you go, carrying this chronic overarousal in your body can lead to many other very real problems.

Not all thoughts about the future are worry. If we anticipate possible negative outcomes calmly, and can generate possible solutions to future problems, we are simply planning or problem solving. However, most anxious thoughts are not so productive. If you aren't generating a list of solutions, you aren't problem solving. If you aren't creating a plan, you aren't planning. Worrying is when thoughts are not productive and instead just lead to even more anxiety. When a person has a pervasive pattern of worry and chronic overarousal that interferes with their ability to function in daily life, they may meet the criteria for a diagnosis of generalized anxiety disorder (GAD). This is when the body has a "high idle" and the mind has the habit of looking for trouble. I think of GAD as a close cousin of OCD, especially the Pure O variety.

OCD and Worry-Like Obsessions

Worry and OCD are very similar in that they are both anxious responses specifically to *thoughts*. Like worry thoughts, the thought part of OCD often takes the form of "What if..." thinking. We can see this pattern in all the examples of obsessive thoughts presented in the introduction: "*What if* there's snot on the jacket?" "*What if* I'm a sociopath?" and "*What if* my son and I grow apart?" Both worry/GAD and OCD can lead to excessive preparation, checking, reassurance seeking, avoidance, and other behaviors that specifically lead to temporary relief from the anxious thoughts. The difference is that in the case of OCD, the thoughts can be a bit more irrational and unrealistic, even to the person thinking them. Also, the anxiety-reducing behaviors can take on a more ritualized form, and their ability to reduce anxiety can have an almost magical or mystical quality. We will discuss this magical element of OCD more fully in the next chapter.

While GAD and OCD are officially classified as two different disorders, I tend to think of them as existing on a continuum. Cognitive fusion is the key, operative factor in both. With GAD, the thoughts are more exclusively focused on possible negative events or outcomes, and the behaviors are more likely to be related in a practical way to the worrisome thought. On the OCD end of the continuum, the anxious thoughts can be more abstract ideas or even images, and the behaviors can be less obviously connected to the thoughts (the magical part). In my experience, many individuals can find themselves operating at either or both ends of this spectrum at any given time. My first book, *The Worry Trap*, focuses more on the GAD end of that spectrum, while this book is more concerned with the OCD end. However, since the problems of excessive worry and obsessing are very similar, the strategies for freeing yourself from the struggle with them are also very much alike. Two types of worry that commonly reach the threshold of obsession are safety concerns and contamination fears. Life presents endless opportunities for obsessing about these two areas, and both can generate a wide range of checking and correcting behaviors that can readily become compulsions. For this reason, safety and contamination fears are probably the most widely recognizable types of OCD.

Safety Concerns

Since anxious thoughts are all about keeping us safe, this category of obsessions is fairly straightforward. These are "What if…" thoughts related to our safety and the safety of others. For example, *What if I forgot to…lock the door? …turn off the stove? …close the windows? …unplug the iron? space heater? toaster? …turn off a burner on the stove? …throw out expired food? …thoroughly clean up broken glass? …securely cap dangerous chemicals or medication? …maintain proper tire pressure in all four wheels?* Whether we place these thoughts at the GAD or OCD end of the spectrum depends on how realistic they are, how pervasive or repetitive they may be, and how often we feel the need to check or reassure ourselves about them.

Excessive concerns about safety happens to be the brand of anxiety that I personally struggle with the most. On a good day, I place myself somewhere near the GAD end of the spectrum, thinking a bit more than the average person about things that might go wrong, and not only being careful to lock the deadbolt on the front door, but then checking to make sure the door I've just locked cannot easily be opened. On a bad day, if I'm feeling more stressed or anxious in general, I can skew sharply toward the OCD end of things, checking the door several times, and maybe even performing a mental ritual like saying "locked" silently to myself.

Sometimes, safety concerns are not just about staying safe. They often have more to do with our personal responsibility in the world. It's not just that we don't want bad things to happen, it's that we don't want them to happen on our watch. This fear of making even small mistakes that could inadvertently lead to harming someone else is often referred to as *scrupulosity*. It can include anything from obsessing about possibly having run over a pedestrian to fears of inadvertently overlooking a hazardous situation like broken glass or a wet, slippery floor. Compulsions related to these thoughts range from checking behaviors to "confessing" small oversights that might create a slight risk for others. In many cases, what drives scrupulosity is not so much a fear of harm as a fear of the guilt one would feel if such harm came to pass.

A child of the 70s, I grew up watching *The Waltons* on TV. The episode I remember most clearly was the one where the Waltons' cozy, white, dormered farmhouse is completely burned out in a raging inferno. Thankfully, every single Walton escapes unsinged (though John-Boy's finished novel is lost to the flames). For the ten-year-old me, far more tragic than the fire, or even the lost novel, was the bitter soul-searching that followed it. John-Boy assumes that the fire was started by the pipe he has recently taken to smoking. At the same time, Grandpa is all but certain that the fire was started by the electric heater he left plugged in following a decadently long bath. We never find out how the fire actually started, but watching John-Boy and Grandpa twist in the bitter winds of their secret guilt and self-recrimination is excruciating. This is often what the person with excessive safety concerns fears most.

In my own case, the anxiety and checking around locking the front door increased sharply when we adopted a sweet but unworldly little cat. My responsibility for keeping her safely inside the house shows up in heightened anxiety around closing and locking the door. To make extra sure I don't slip up, my brain sends me thoughts about the door being left ajar, or blowing open in a strong wind. There's a narrative there, not just about the cat getting out, but about it being my fault. I could end up like John-Boy or Grandpa, buried by guilt. When I'm feeling anxious, cognitive fusion leads me to experience this narrative as not merely possible, but likely. It also results in a strong feeling that the door I have just locked and checked may, in fact, still be unlocked.

Contamination Fears

Even before germ theory became widely accepted in the nineteenth century, people from all cultures expressed fears of contamination of various sorts. People or animals were considered unclean in various circumstances and at different times. Ritualistic bathing or token handwashing was a required part of certain religious practices. Today, most of us learn about germs at an early age, from parents and then from teachers. We learn to fear contact with germs and to follow rules of good hygiene like washing our hands, bathing, and brushing our teeth. We are taught to cover our mouth and nose when we sneeze or cough, and to avoid other people's bodily fluids. We also learn rules about safe food preparation and storage. The degree of focus on germs as well as the emphasis on these rules can vary considerably between different cultures and from one family to the next. This ambiguity about exactly what is safe and how much cleanliness is required, combined with the implication of potentially serious consequences for missteps, makes this area ripe for both obsessions and compulsions.

The COVID-19 pandemic offered many people who were previously not so concerned about contamination a clearer understanding of the anxiety that people with obsessive contamination fears face every day. Surprisingly, I found that some of my patients with this sort of OCD were less thrown by COVID concerns than the average person, in many cases because they were already taking precautions that were new to everyone else. Others, who had made progress on reducing handwashing and not avoiding perceived contaminants, suddenly had trouble knowing where to draw the line between reasonable precautions and OCD behavior. Early in the pandemic, when there was limited understanding of how the virus was transmitted, I found it difficult to offer much guidance in this area. I was too busy washing my hands and wiping down doorknobs.

For many people with contamination fears, the focus centers on *fomites*—any objects that might be a conduit for germs passing from one person to another. Think faucet handles, elevator buttons, shopping carts, public mailboxes, and every surface in the public transit system. While many of us are aware of the potential for contamination these items pose and reduce the risk by washing our hands before eating (and perhaps even more regularly during flu season or a global pandemic), for the person with OCD, the experience is a little different. When anxiety about contamination is particularly high, touching a fomite leads not only to thoughts about contamination, but, thanks to cognitive fusion, to an intense *feeling* that one is contaminated. Patients regularly report that until they wash it, the hand that touched the doorknob *feels* different than the one that did not.

Another focus of concern is often contact with blood or fecal matter. While there may be limited opportunities for this in daily life, it depends on how you define "contact." For individuals with this brand of OCD, stepping on a dried smudge of what *might* be feces on the sidewalk, even when wearing thick-soled shoes, qualifies as contact. For Anthony, just smelling poo qualified as contact and contamination. A devoted urban jogger, whenever he came across one of those portable toilets on the sidewalk in front of every construction site, he routinely ran out into the street to avoid being contaminated by the toilet's smell. Only when he was almost hit by a passing truck did he begin to suspect that his anxious brain was protecting him from the wrong thing.

OCD can also take the form of contamination fears that are only indirectly about germs. This can lead to avoiding people or settings that are just generally perceived as dirty or gross. Compulsions associated with this contact often go beyond handwashing and can include showering and washing or even discarding clothing worn during the encounter. Anthony's obsessing and avoidance of the sneezed-on jacket are an example of this "emotional contamination." Here, the focus is not so much on washing away germs. Instead, the washing is a ritualized attempt to remove the thoughts and feelings of contamination produced by cognitive fusion.

Common "Pure O" Obsessions

It's when we are literally afraid of a thought that we experience cognitive fusion in its most explicit form. When this is the case, any struggle to stop or change our thoughts can lead to more anxiety, and therefore more fusion. This *obsessive cycle* is a positive feedback loop that can lead to rapidly escalating anxiety. In this Pure O pattern of OCD, the compulsive behavior may not be readily apparent. As mentioned earlier, it could be avoidance, very subtle behaviors meant to give reassurance, or an invisible thought-based ritual. Subtle or not, the compulsions play a key role in reinforcing and maintaining the obsessive cycle. While Pure O can take on an unlimited variety of forms, there are several common patterns.

Intrusive Thoughts and Images

Sometimes thoughts that become obsessions are less like a narrative and more like a bumper sticker or pop-up ad. It may be an emotionally loaded word or phrase or a disturbing image that repeatedly comes to mind, eliciting a startle response and an immediate struggle to avoid or banish the thought. Sometimes it's a thought that encapsulates broader negative beliefs, like the word "loser." Other times, it's an unpleasant memory from the past, like the image of a loved one in pain or a gory scene from a movie. For religious individuals, it can be blasphemous phrases or images. What all of these thoughts have in common is that the person finds them unpleasant and would prefer not to think them. Because of this, they may respond to the thoughts with resistance, trying to push them away, especially if they see the thoughts as a threat. Because resistance and pushing involve an increased fight-or-flight response, this struggle only leads to more stickiness. It's another instance of trying to force the gorilla out of the room, with the result of keeping the gorilla in the room. It's all the pushing against a thought that leads us to experience it as dangerous or intrusive. A good definition of an obsession is "a thought you are not willing to have." If you're not struggling to stop or control a thought, it's not really an obsession…it's just a thought.

"Harm OCD"

It's not unusual for intrusive thoughts to include violent imagery, like thoughts of stabbing or bludgeoning loved ones or family pets. The thoughts may be sexual in nature, especially thoughts of acts that run counter to the individual's morals or values. Part of the anxiety associated with these "bad thoughts" is the accompanying idea that they might represent secret urges or desires and the individual's fear that they may act on them. One way to understand these thoughts is as a warning message from the anxious part of the brain. Like the thoughts of jumping that occur when we are in a high place, which is the brain's way of saying, "Don't jump," violent or inappropriate sexual images are a similar, though unwelcome, reminder from the brain that "this would be a bad thing to do." It's impossible to have a thought about *not* doing something that doesn't include a thought about the thing you don't want to do.

Our brain actually sends us warnings and reminders like this all the time. Let's say you decide to make a salad. You rinse a tomato and grab a sharp knife. From the moment you pick up the knife, if you're paying close attention, you'll notice thoughts about the sharpness of the knife, and maybe even fleeting images of cutting yourself or anyone standing nearby with the knife. You respond to these thoughts and images by handling the knife differently than you would handle a spoon or some other less dangerous object. As you begin to slice the tomato, if you pay close attention, you'll notice the idea or image coming to mind of slicing through one of your fingers. You respond to this thought by carefully positioning your fingers outside the path of the slicing knife. These thoughts are simply your brain doing its job of protecting you.

Now, if, you happen to have a high level of anxiety about knives, or a fear of slicing off your fingers, cognitive fusion might lead you to experience these normal thoughts as *urges* to slice off your finger, or to stab or cut someone. This could lead you to look for and push against or try to get rid of these thoughts when you're handling a knife. As your anxiety increased, your brain would send more warnings, resulting in a struggle and the perception that the thoughts were intrusive and uncontrollable. Normal thoughts about the danger of sharp knives would become obsessive and fraught with anxiety. You might respond to this by compulsively avoiding knives, hiding them, or even removing them from your kitchen. You might feel compelled to confess to your roommate that you sometimes have thoughts of stabbing her. While these compulsions might reduce your anxiety in the short term, in the long term, they serve to reinforce and maintain the fear. Avoiding knives would prevent you from learning that controlling your thoughts when handling a knife has nothing to do with controlling the actual knife. In addition, the compulsions would likely lead to other, more practical problems in the world outside of your thoughts. For example, it may be difficult to prepare a meal without using a knife, and your roommate might be upset to hear that you're thinking of stabbing her.

Needing to Be Certain

Another common pattern of obsessive thinking has to do with our response to ambiguity or uncertainty. In nature, ambiguity represents a threat. If we don't know what's coming toward us through the bushes, we're less likely to be prepared for it. Because of this, we've learned to fear what is unknown or unclear and to respond to it by trying to reduce the ambiguity. For people with OCD, this can take the form of obsessing about things that are less than clear. This can play a role in safety or contamination obsessions, as in *How can I be sure the door is locked?* or *What was that smudge I saw on the sidewalk?* The need to be certain is also at work when we feel the need to reread a paragraph just in case we missed an important sentence or word, or to ask someone to repeat what they said earlier, in case we misunderstood or forgot something important.

Certain types of human experience are inherently ambiguous and hard to pin down. One is the meaning of subtle social cues, as mentioned in the section on social anxiety. Another is our feelings about other people. Feelings wax and wane from day to day, and even when we love someone deeply, we do not constantly feel that love in the same way. Sophie's obsessing about her feelings for her parents is an example of the need to be certain. Something is changing in Sophie's relationship with her parents. To us, it may look like a healthy maturing into more independence and involvement with her own, increasingly adult life. Sophie's not so sure. One of her greatest fears is to lose the special connection she feels to her parents. Just the idea that it might not be there makes her anxious. She responds to this fear by checking to see if she has the "right" level of feeling about her parents. Unlike checking your pocket for your car keys, it can be a little unclear what we are feeling, or how strongly we are feeling it at a given moment. This ambiguity only increases Sophie's anxiety. The thought ritual of imagining her parents' funeral as a way to reassure herself only leads to more questions. The only thing harder than knowing exactly how we feel right now is predicting exactly how we will feel in an imagined future.

Cognitive fusion comes into play when the brain attempts to reduce our uncertainty. Since "sitting with" the ambiguity of not knowing what's coming through the bushes can lead to being devoured, the anxious brain gives us the illusion of certainty. We "know" it's a tiger, even if we really don't. It's natural for the mind to respond to ambiguity with *Maybe it's this* or *Maybe it's that*. Cognitive fusion leads us to experience these thoughts as *It IS this or that*. Sophie's mind offers her a possible explanation for her ambiguous feelings about her parents: *Maybe you're a sociopath*. Her anxiety leads her to experience this thought in a fused way: the very presence of the thought suggests that it could be true. As anxiety about the thought increases, so does fusion, making it "feel" even more true. This fused "feeling" carries more weight for Sophie than the contradictory evidence that she is crying at the very possibility of not loving her parents. For those of us standing outside of her obsessive cycle, Sophie's concern and her tears are all the evidence we need to conclude that she loves her parents dearly.

"Relationship OCD" and "Sexual Orientation OCD"

The ambiguity inherent in our feelings for others, as well as a similar fuzziness surrounding feelings of physical attraction, contributes to two types of OCD that have received increased attention in recent years. While not official diagnoses, "relationship OCD" and "sexual orientation OCD" are well documented and much discussed in online forums.

Relationship OCD involves a low tolerance for any uncertainty about our choice of intimate partner. Often the obsessive component is an amplified version of the old question "Is this the right person for me?" Other times, it can take the form of obsessing about our partner's physical imperfections or perceived shortcomings. Compulsive responses to these thoughts might include avoiding making a long-term commitment to the relationship or avoiding looking at a partner. These obsessions go beyond the pet peeves that most of us develop about a partner. For example, one patient of mine became so fixated on what he considered his girlfriend's gratingly unpleasant laugh that he fled the room when he heard it. He refused to watch any funny movies or television shows with her, and eventually began to avoid saying anything she might find humorous, being careful to maintain a neutral and morose attitude in her presence. Relationship OCD can also include obsessions about a partner's sexual history or about their fidelity or future fidelity. Here, the not-so-subtle rituals might include relentless questioning and interrogation of a partner about their sexual history or attractions to others. I worked with one young man who routinely asked his wife if she had had sex with any of their neighbors, with the mailman, or with the doorman in their building. Surprisingly, he was usually satisfied when she answered these questions with a simple "no," but then repeated the questions again days later "in case anything had changed." His ready acceptance of her answers and the irrational repetition of the questions betrays that this is a ritual. He didn't believe it was likely that she had been unfaithful, it just *felt* likely. Engaging in the ritual of questions and answers offered temporary relief from that feeling. In rituals like this, you can actually hear the irrational part of the brain at work. He once asked if, in her past, she had ever performed in an adult film. When she assured him that she had not, he asked if it was possible that she had done so and then forgotten about it!

Fans of the sitcom classic *Seinfeld* will likely remember the episode in which George, anxious about receiving a massage from a male masseur, subsequently obsesses about whether or not "it moved" during the massage, adding, "It was imperceptible, but I felt it!." Individuals with sexual orientation OCD, or what has also been called "gay OCD," obsess about their sexual orientation. While these individuals do not enjoy sexual fantasies about members of the same sex, and in fact desire and enjoy sex with members of the opposite sex, they are uncomfortable with the very possibility that they may, on some level, be gay, or might at some time in the future become gay. The problem with this low tolerance for uncertainty is that sexual attraction, like other preferences, always includes a degree of ambiguity. What if a man is attracted to a woman who is slightly masculine? What does it mean to recognize a member of the same sex as "objectively" attractive? Is it significant that if you were forced to choose a same-sex partner, you would prefer one person over another? Incidentally, while it's less common, a similar dilemma can occur for the person who identifies as gay or lesbian but has obsessive concerns that they may actually be straight. After coming out to family members and friends, and perhaps building a long-term relationship with a same-sex partner, discovering that you are in fact straight could indeed be inconvenient in a number of ways.

Compulsive responses to obsessive questioning of sexual orientation usually include some sort of "checking" to test whether or not one feels attracted to a given person, or if imagining having sex with them is arousing. The problem with this is that not only can human beings imagine doing almost anything, but we can also imagine enjoying doing it. However, imagining enjoying something is not the same thing as enjoying it. For example, if you look at a wall in the room you're sitting in, you can probably imagine what it would be like to walk over to the wall and give it a good lick…with your tongue. Even though you may never have licked a wall before, you can probably imagine, with some accuracy, what this would be like…right? Not only that…if you try just a little bit, you can probably also imagine enjoying it. Go ahead and try to imagine that. Imagine that you just *loved* licking that wall. You can probably imagine enjoying it so much that you want to lick the wall extensively, or maybe try licking other walls, in other rooms. Can you imagine that? Of course you can. Now, the question is…does that make you, on some level, an avid wall-licker? If you haven't acted on these thoughts, could you nonetheless perhaps be a repressed wall-licker? Is there a difference between wanting or liking something and *imagining* that we want or like something? When cognitive fusion comes into play, the answer is "I'm not sure."

Maximizing or FOMO

Given a choice between something good and something better, most of us would choose the something better. Because we have an aversion to losing things, we can even have something good and experience the lack of something better as a loss. Because we have good imaginations, we can do this even if we haven't experienced something better, and even if we are not completely certain that something better exists. Cognitive fusion only makes the something better seem more real, or only slightly beyond our reach...intensifying the sense of loss. Psychologist Barry Schwartz, who has done extensive research on this phenomenon and its implications for mental health and economics, refers to the impulse to have the best possible thing as "maximizing" (B. Schwartz et al. 2002).

But how do we know that we have the best possible thing? What if there is something better out there? These questions naturally arise when considering our choice of romantic partner, a job or career, which school to attend or send our children to, where to go or where to stay on a vacation, where to live, which restaurant to try, or even what to order from the menu. Notably, this is a predicament more often faced in affluent societies where a multitude of options are available in all of these areas. The anxiety that accompanies this abundance of choice has come to be known as FOMO: *Fear Of Missing Out*. For many people, it is also a fear of regret. We imagine our future selves discovering a better option than the one we chose. The indecision and struggle produced by maximizing and FOMO has its own trendy name: *analysis paralysis*.

In his research on maximizing, Dr. Schwartz has found that people who tend to be the greatest maximizers not only take the longest time to decide, but also are less satisfied with their choices, less happy, and less optimistic than people with low maximization scores. He goes on to suggest that, while initially having increased choices makes us feel better, at some point, increased choice actually decreases our happiness. He explains this in terms of "opportunity costs." Since the choice of one thing means the loss of another, as options increase, so does the sense of loss that comes with our ultimate decision (B. Schwartz 2004). Since those "lost opportunities" exist only as thoughts, however, it's likely that cognitive fusion plays an important role in this experience of loss, and in the anxiety surrounding making choices. We will look more closely at how cognitive fusion contributes to analysis paralysis in chapter four.

From Cognitive Fusion to Defusion— A Look Ahead

In this chapter, we set out to consider the great variety of ways that cognitive fusion can lead us to respond to our own thoughts in problematic ways. We looked at the thinking or narrative component of common phobias and how a desire to avoid similar narratives or stories is at the heart of OCD, and especially Pure O. Social anxiety and feelings of being "not good enough" offer good examples of how sticky narratives can "feel true" even in the absence of any supporting evidence. We discussed the close association of chronic worry or generalized anxiety disorder and OCD in that both involve anxious responses to thoughts, and I offered my argument for placing these two disorders on a continuum. Finally, we went over a list of common forms of the Pure O pattern of OCD, noting that it is the increased stickiness of thoughts, rather than the thoughts themselves, that is problematic. In other words, it's not the *content* of the thought, but our relationship to that thought, and our response to it, that causes us to suffer.

To the extent that cognitive fusion plays a central role in all the problems outlined here, *cognitive defusion* can offer a path to decreased struggling and suffering in all of these areas. As used here, the word "defusion" is not about directly reducing danger or tension, as in "defusing the situation," but rather about de-fusing, or separating a thought from the reality that it refers to. Part two of this book is all about how to accomplish this. Before you skip ahead to those chapters, however, it's important to have a firm grasp on what cognitive fusion is and to be able to recognize the many forms that it can take. A prerequisite of de-fusing things is recognizing that they are fused in the first place. In fact, one of the easiest ways to achieve defusion is by simply recognizing and identifying fusion when it's happening. I call this skill *Labeling*. It is the first, and most important, of the five skills presented in part two. The next three chapters describe three important areas where cognitive fusion comes into play, especially where OCD is concerned: magical thinking, thoughts of the past or future, and your sense of self.

CHAPTER 3

As Above, So Below

Magic...we have all wanted it at some point. Whether it's crossing our fingers, wishing upon a star, or searching for that four-leaf clover, most of us have yearned for the power and protection of magic. And no, not just as children. Even in our most adult moments, we have wanted to just make it happen, to make it okay...with the power of thinking it so.

Study Habits

Judy had always been a good student. In high school, good grades came fairly easily for her. Then, she barely studied and still did well on tests. Now, in the middle of her college career, things were much more difficult for some reason. It wasn't that she found the material more challenging so much as that the stakes seemed so much higher. Making sure she did well required more work and more control of all the variables.

The focus tonight was on preparing for tomorrow's history exam. It was a midterm, so there was a lot to cover. Judy started the evening by preparing her customary pre-test meal of cheese toast, being careful to cut the slices of bread diagonally, then eating them slowly at her desk while skimming through the highlighted sections of her textbook. When she came to the end of a section or chapter, she noted the page number. If it was an even number, she moved on to the next section. If it was an odd number, she looked at the clock on her desk. If the minute hand was close to landing on an even number, she would just watch it, waiting for the hand to line up with the even number, swallow once, then continue with her reading. If she had just missed an even number, say it was thirty-one minutes after the hour, and she would have to wait nine minutes until the big hand was on the eight to continue, she could compensate for the odd feeling by clearing her throat an even number of times, usually four, but sometimes six or eight, then looking back at the text and starting to read again.

This system worked fine as long as it wasn't interrupted. Not being interrupted was the reason Judy had a private room in the dorm. Still, sometimes she heard her neighbors through the wall, or a commotion out in the hall. This was not a problem if it was just low talking or music. If it was something unexpected, however, like a knocking sound, or especially a sneeze or cough, she would have to stop studying altogether. When this happened, she usually took a short break, going to the bathroom or just pacing up and down the hallway for a bit, trying to look casual. When she came back to start again, she tried to just naturally enter the room on her right foot, but sometimes she had to step in and out of the room a couple of times to get it right. Once she was at her desk again, she looked at the clock and either waited for an even number or did the throat clearing again before getting back to the text. Being disciplined and studying like this was a lot of work, but so far, it was paying off.

OCD and Sympathetic Magic

Compared to the examples of OCD discussed so far, Judy's compulsions are more obvious and have a more ritualistic quality. In fact, the compulsive part of Judy's OCD is more apparent and easier to identify than the obsessive part. In her case, the obsessions are rather vague but nonetheless fused thoughts about doing poorly on the history test or not getting good grades in general. These thoughts and the anxiety associated with them are momentarily dispelled by her complex rituals. What you may have noticed is that those rituals have no clear connection to studying. In fact, they seem to be largely incompatible with studying, which would seem to be an important part of doing well on the test. The only apparent function of the rituals is to reduce Judy's anxiety. That is what *we* see. In Judy's experience, however, controlling all the variables through her rituals is actually part of controlling how well she does on the history test. Starting out on the "right" foot and aligning her studying with even numbers to counteract "odd" feelings is connected, for Judy, to getting an A.

Now, if you were to ask Judy if she *really believes* that stepping into a room with her left foot or ignoring the numbers on a clock could lead to her failing an exam, she would probably say no. People with OCD usually recognize such rituals as excessive and probably unnecessary. However, Judy would likely argue that in spite of *knowing* the rituals aren't connected to her performance on the test, in the moment it very strongly *feels* like they are. That's because the rituals act to counter Judy's thoughts about performing poorly, and, while she knows these are just thoughts, cognitive fusion leads them to feel like something more. This chapter is all about the role of rituals in OCD and their connection to cognitive fusion. Rituals usually play an important role in strengthening and maintaining OCD, and not just the more obvious kind that consume so much of Judy's time and energy. More subtle, "invisible" rituals are often a significant part of "Pure O" OCD as well.

What makes something a ritual is that it is done in one setting, or on one level, to affect outcomes in another setting, or on another level. We control *this* to control *that*. Judy controls her interactions with the page numbers and clock numbers *here* to control her performance on the history test *there*. In OCD, rituals often involve counting, symmetry, order, and approximations of "perfection" on a local level aimed at creating a corresponding order in the larger world. In a more immediate sense, the ritual is actually an effort to dispel or control anxious *thoughts* about a negative outcome. This experience that controlling these thoughts is the same thing as controlling the future outcome is an example of cognitive fusion.

Ritualized actions performed on one level to control outcomes on another level, in the absence of a clear causal connection between the two, are also associated with certain mystical rites and magic. *Sympathetic magic,* also known as "imitative magic" or "contagious magic," refers to this correspondence between two seemingly unrelated things. This implied correspondence between one realm and another is also captured neatly in the words "as above, so below," a phrase attributed to early mystical writers and associated with alchemy. Ritual substitutes one thing from this realm for another, from that realm. I like to use the term "rain dance" to illustrate this concept, keeping in mind the rich history behind this complex cultural ritual common among some Indigenous Peoples. In early agrarian societies, when this ritual originated, what was needed to make the wheat grow tall was rain. However, nobody could directly control *that*. What was in their control was *this:* dancing. Rain dances, which often simulated the movement of wheat waving in the wind, were an effort to control *that* by controlling *this*. Today, while rain dances may be performed as a valued part of some Indigenous Peoples' heritage, they tend not to be relied upon to irrigate crops.

When we look at Judy's rituals as an effort to influence her performance on the test, we can think of her clock watching and throat clearing as a sort of rain dance. Even though Judy is a good student and consistently puts in the work necessary to make success likely, that success is never completely guaranteed. The uncertainty that remains leads to feelings of anxiety. Judy's rituals provide a sense of increased control over the ultimate outcome of events, which temporarily reduces her anxiety. This understanding of the connection between uncertainty, anxiety, and rituals is based largely on the research and writing of the cultural anthropologist Bronislaw Malinowski (Homans 1941). An expert on rituals of all kinds, he lived with and studied the cultural life of the Trobriand Islanders in New Guinea during the 1920s. Based on his observations there and elsewhere, he concluded that the performance of rituals increases in response to perceived uncertainty. The less control we feel we have, the more likely we are to engage in some sort of ritual. His argument went something like this: People hold a body of practical knowledge, which they can apply to get the results they desire. They do so when planting crops, catching fish, or taking history tests. However, even with their best efforts, a certain degree of uncertainty remains. There may be a drought, the locusts may come, the fish may just not be biting. This uncertainty creates anxiety. The ritual provides a sense of increased control and reduces the anxiety. He offered the following illustration of this correlation between uncertainty and ritual from his observation of Trobriand fishermen:

In the lagoon fishing, where man can rely completely upon his knowledge and skill, magic does not exist, while in the open-sea fishing, full of danger and uncertainty, there is extensive magical ritual to secure safety and good results. (Homans 1941, 30–31)

The magical "as above, so below" quality we see in Judy's complex ritual is less obvious in the covert rituals in Pure O patterns of OCD. While responses like subtle avoidance or mental operations are not observable in the way that Judy's rituals are, they are still efforts to control thoughts, often about future outcomes. When we experience these thoughts in a fused way, effort to control those thoughts amounts to efforts to control those outcomes. This was the case for Lou, whose story you read in the introduction. Lou's obsessions focus on an outcome that may or may not happen in the future: his son may or may not grow more distant from him as he grows up. It's impossible for Lou to completely predict or control whether or not this will happen, and the uncertainty about the outcome makes him anxious. Since he can't completely control the future of his relationship with Adam, Lou instead attempts to control his thoughts about it. When he sees the sappy commercial about a child going off to college, he changes the channel. Ultimately, he begins to avoid his son. For Lou, as for Judy, these responses can be seen as an attempt to control events and outcomes in the real world by controlling thoughts in the analog world of the mind. Remember that thoughts, like all language, are symbols. One thing, here, substituted for another thing, there. Obsessive thoughts are to OCD what the stars are to astrology. The experience that controlling *this* (thoughts) will control *that* (reality) is an expression of cognitive fusion. The thoughts, and the reality they refer to, are *fused* in our experience. We may not *believe* they are the same thing, but we respond as if they are.

Most people with OCD do not believe that stepping on a crack will actually break their mother's back. The perceived power lies not so much in the crack-stepping as in the incantation itself. The *thought* that stepping on a crack will break your mother's back is the danger. Avoiding cracks is a way of avoiding that dangerous thought. I once saw a young man in my practice who was convinced that exerting control over his thoughts was imperative not only to his mother's back, but to the safety and well-being of all of his loved ones, and even that of complete strangers. His rituals for "neutralizing" dangerous thoughts involved slowing or freezing his movements until the thoughts could be dismissed as harmless. It could take him five to ten minutes to get from the door of my office to his seat. Once, after spending several minutes "frozen" in the middle of the room, he reported that a thought had popped into his head about children trapped in a burning building. By freezing and neutralizing this thought, he maintained that he might have saved the lives of several unidentified children "somewhere." When I asked if he really believed this was the case, he acknowledged that it was very unlikely. However, he insisted that, with the lives of innocent children at stake, he "couldn't take the chance" of just ignoring the thought.

While complex OCD rituals, like primitive magic, may seem rather exotic, they are actually not so different from many accepted practices in our culture. After finishing a sentence that starts with the word "Hopefully," do you ever "knock on wood"? This is an example of not only a ritual, but an incantation or "spell," using words ("Hopefully...") to influence events. Have you ever tossed salt over your shoulder after spilling it? When's the last time you intentionally walked under a ladder when it was possible to go around it? Would you perhaps avoid scheduling an important event like a house closing or a wedding on Friday the 13th? If you don't subscribe to these rituals, you likely know people who do. Widely held superstitions like these owe their origins to the same process of anxiety and cognitive fusion underlying the more bespoke versions that are part of OCD.

Dualism and Idealism

The basic notion of a causal connection between thoughts and reality has held a central place in the human experience for millennia. The construction of two separate but corresponding worlds, one of mind, the other of matter, is referred to in philosophy as *dualism.* Some have argued that, for early people, objects of thought or imagination were in some ways more important and enduring than objects in the world, which were seen as more temporary and subject to change. "Eternal truths" existed in the mind, while reality was "an illusion."

The Cave

The dualistic worldview is clearly formulated and expressed in Plato's allegory "The Cave." According to Plato, our position in the world is similar to that of people living their whole lives inside a cave. The sun is shining outside, but we are always facing the back wall of the cave. When things happen outside, and objects or other creatures pass by the mouth of the cave, their shadows are cast onto this back wall. In our cave-bound ignorance, we take these shadows to be the whole of reality. In this metaphor, the world outside of the cave represents the "higher reality" of thoughts and ideas. The material world that we perceive as real is actually just a shadow cast by the more enduring realm of ideas.

The implication of this worldview is that the best way to change or influence events in the material (shadow) world is by changing or controlling events in the thought world (outside the cave). Sound familiar? Most forms of OCD, and Pure O in particular, can be seen as a manifestation of this worldview, even if only temporarily or in a limited scope. The notion that ideas are more real or more important than the physical objects they refer to has been called *idealism,* as in "The Platonic Ideal." If this sounds like the opposite of how we usually think about reality, it is. Contrary to the idealism that may have prevailed early on, *materialism* is the dominant paradigm of day-to-day thinking for most people in the modern world. Materialism asserts that matter precedes ideas. First there is the object, then there is our idea of it. Idealism asserts that the idea comes first. While each of us may hold a wide variety of beliefs about the power of thoughts or the ultimate nature of reality in general, most of us do not rely on magic to get us through the day. We may say a quick prayer before getting on the freeway, but we also buckle our seatbelts.

Cognitive Fusion and Idealism

The early emergence of a dualistic worldview makes sense when you consider the parallel way that human beings experience things. On the outside, we experience objects and events in the current moment through our senses. We *see* a goat in the meadow, we *feel* its straw-like hair, we *hear* its bleating, we *taste* its milk, and we *smell* its goatiness. Later, lying in bed, we close our eyes and remember the goat. We can kind of see it, feel it, even smell it…but when we open our eyes, there's no goat there. Our experience is of two worlds. The outside world, which exists in the moment, and the inside world, which lasts beyond the moment. In the morning, if we're hungry, we might think of the goat and remember the milk. If we follow these thoughts, they will guide us to breakfast. The thoughts correspond to the outside world, and they have power.

Still, most of the time we know that we cannot milk the "inside goat" of our thoughts. If we're hungry, we have to find an "outside goat." At other times, though, this separation of inside and outside can become murkier. On another night, lying in bed, when we think about our favorite goat, sleeping in the meadow, we might also think about the wolves we have heard howling in the forest. Our ancient, anxious brain knows all about wolves and goats, so it sends us a warning image, an "inside wolf," in the meadow, stalking our favorite goat. If we're a bit keyed up, and maybe already having some trouble falling asleep, the inside wolf and the outside wolf can become one and the same. Fused. In response, our heart rate and blood pressure rise, and our muscles tighten. Our body is preparing to save our favorite goat!

We might respond to this by getting up and running to the meadow. If we find our favorite goat sleeping peacefully there, we are reassured. Back in bed, the inside wolf is nowhere to be seen. If we get tired of all this late-night running to the meadow, we might discover that it's easier to get rid of the inside wolf by quietly saying the words "Not by the hair of my chinny-chin-chin." If saying it once doesn't work, three times in a row might do the trick. Over time, this becomes a ritual, or a spell that keeps the inside wolf, and by extension, the outside wolf, at bay. "Hopefully…there won't be any wolves in the meadow." Knock on wood.

Idealism as a Cultural Movement

While a more materialistic perspective has come to dominate modern culture, idealism is far from dead. In 2006, Australian television producer Rhonda Byrne, whose former credits included *Oz Encounters: UFOs in Australia* and *The World's Greatest Commercials*, published *The Secret,* a self-help book that has sold 30 million copies worldwide, been translated into fifty languages, and praised by Oprah. The book has spawned several sequels and an array of *The Secret* merchandise. The book's premise, which is no longer much of a secret, is that our thoughts about certain things have the power to manifest or create those things in our lives. It emphasizes the practice of visualizing the things you wish to bring into your life. Byrne credits the thinking of Edwardian writer Wallace Wattles as her inspiration for *The Secret.* His book, *The Science of Getting Rich,* published in 1910, and a related book entitled *Thought Vibration or The Law of Attraction in the Thought World* by William Walker Atkinson were both products of the "New Thought" movement, which was popular in the US in the mid-nineteenth century. Byrne repopularized Atkinson's term "the law of attraction." The origins of New Thought can be traced back further to the writings of the mental healer Phineas Quimby, who maintained that all physical illness originated in the mind. Quimby treated and influenced the thinking of Mary Baker Eddy, who founded Christian Science.

Whether old or new, "secret" or heavily marketed brand, a primary criticism of this line of thinking is that it blames the victim. If you fail to get rich, or otherwise manifest an abundance of good things in your life, the problem lies with you and your stinkin' thinkin'. If your life is blighted by poverty, illness, or disability, well…it's a shame you couldn't think up something a little better for yourself. Conversely, it attributes all of the credit for what might otherwise be seen as good luck to those who have ended up with more than their share of life's bounty. Your personal jet and ocean-front estate only prove what an evolved thinker and adept visual-izer you must be. When you consider this persisting cultural messaging about the magical "power of thoughts" and our inclinations as a species toward cognitive fusion, it's not surprising that the idea of treating thoughts as "just thoughts" meets a certain amount of resistance, especially from people with OCD.

Religious Beliefs and OCD

The idea that thoughts make all the difference is not strictly the provenance of Victorian spiritualists and New Age TV producers. Many traditional religions have also emphasized the importance of thinking "good thoughts." Prayer often takes the form of thoughts, and most religions view rituals as significant and powerful. For individuals struggling with OCD who also happen to be religious, it can be difficult to know where to draw the line between their religious beliefs and their OCD. Is it possible to practice cognitive defusion and maintain one's religious belief and devotions? In my experience, this confusion often shows up in two common patterns of OCD. In the first, intrusive thoughts are seen as blasphemous or otherwise going against an individual's morals or religious beliefs. Struggling to eliminate or control those thoughts can be seen as an act of religious obligation. The other form is when a religious practice, like saying a prayer or making the sign of the cross, has become an OCD ritual. In both cases, I have found it helpful to ask patients about how they distinguish between religious beliefs and superstition, and whether superstition can sometimes show up in the guise of religious beliefs.

Malinowski made a distinction between magical and religious rituals. In his view, a magical rite had a clear and definite practical purpose: a good crop yield, the catching of many fish, and so on. He maintained that this was not true of most religious rituals, which were intended to show devotion or elicit more general well-being or protection. This distinction was criticized by other anthropologists (Homans 1941) and may be harder to see in some cases than in others. I believe a similar, though equally blurry, distinction can be made between religious rituals and superstition, with OCD being more like superstition. In OCD, individuals are usually focused on controlling specific outcomes through their own behavior, while in religious rituals and prayer, they are appealing to a higher power to intervene on their behalf. Belief in the necessity of OCD rituals varies depending on a person's level of anxiety, while spiritual and religious beliefs tend to be much more constant.

When this sort of confusion has arisen with religious patients with OCD, I have on occasion found it helpful to involve the patient's priest or rabbi in the discussion. I've found that such religious leaders tend to make clear distinctions between religious practice and what they see as superstition, and can help patients feel better about letting go of certain rituals or their struggles to control certain thoughts. In one case, I worked with a Catholic woman who was having intrusive thoughts about Jesus that she saw as blasphemous and felt obligated by her faith to suppress and struggle against these thoughts. After her priest assured her that the mere presence of these thoughts was not a sin and that it would be okay to accept and "lean into" these thoughts as part of our treatment plan, she was able to do so and achieved a great deal of relief.

Understanding and Noticing Fusion

Recognizing efforts to manage outcomes in the real world by controlling your thoughts or by engaging in rituals as magical thinking can be an important first step toward cognitive defusion. Whatever our religious or spiritual beliefs, and in spite of evidence from the field of quantum physics for as-yet-unidentified connections between consciousness and matter, most of us think and operate in a materialistic, nonmagical way most of the time. In my experience, most people with OCD maintain that they do not actually believe in magic as the best way to influence things like test performance, health and safety, or the future of their relationships. In my practice, I have found that labeling compulsive actions like rituals, checking, reassurance seeking, and even avoidance as "rain dances," "spells," and "magic" can increase an individual's awareness of what they are doing or attempting to do. Becoming more aware that we are operating solely on a symbolic level is itself a form of defusion.

Remember my personal experience of checking and rechecking that locked front door while saying the word "locked" to myself? When I identified and labeled this practice as "casting a spell" on the door to assure that it stayed locked, it was suddenly easier for me to abandon at least the "locked" part of this ritual. When Judy began to think of her pre-exam rituals as a "rain dance" to bring good grades, she was more aware of the disconnected, magical nature of trying to control *that* by controlling *this*. It made the distinction between studying, which actually prepared her for the test, and the rituals, which were only aimed at the thoughts, more apparent. This understanding made it easier for her to experiment with letting the anxious thoughts stick around, relaxing the throat clearing and putting the clock away, even as she continued to study. For Lou, understanding the "as above, so below" quality of trying to control his thoughts about his son made him more aware that the son of his thoughts was not the same as the flesh-and-blood son in his life. Efforts to manage and control his relationship with the "inside son" came at a cost to his relationship with the real one. Making this distinction made it easier for him to act on his values and commit to spending more time with the "outside son," allowing the "inside son" to do whatever he wished. In the second part of this book, we will look more closely at the power of labeling cognitive fusion when it is happening and explore a variety of ways to create more separation between our experience of what is above and what is below.

CHAPTER 4

The Arrow of Time

We have heard that we must live with the past. This is true, and we must live with the future as well. We live with both past and future as they exist in our minds, entirely in the present. Only the present moment is available to us as a direct experience. We experience both the past and the future exclusively as thoughts. Like all thoughts, both memories of the past and images of the future are susceptible to cognitive fusion. When we find ourselves struggling to alter events that occurred in the past or dreading a possible future as fixed and inevitable, we are experiencing what I like to call "time fusion." This extremely cool-sounding subtype of cognitive fusion plays a key role in the obsessive indecision of analysis paralysis and in obsessive regret.

Opportunity Knocks Twice

Miguel could not decide. Suddenly, after being unhappy in his job for the past five years, he had the opportunity to leave for something better. His girlfriend, Rita, had convinced him to finally apply for a position with a large company in the city. To his surprise, he had sailed through the interview process and was now sitting on an offer that included a significant increase in salary and lots of potential for growth. The commute into the city from their home in the suburbs would be grueling, but he was ready for a change. Then, before he could decide whether or not to ask about working from home some days, he got a call from Gil, a former coworker who was now at a small company right in Miguel's neighborhood. There was an opening on the team Gil managed, and he wanted to hire Miguel! Gil's smaller company could not quite match the salary offer of the big firm, and there wasn't quite the opportunity for growth. However, Gil raved about the laid-back, family-like culture there and assured Miguel that he would have complete control over his work schedule.

Miguel made a list of the pros and cons. Option one: more money and room to move up, but as a cog in a big machine, with a brutal commute. Option two: less money and less growth, but cool coworkers and no commute. No matter how many times he did the math, both options came out equally attractive, though for different reasons. There was no clear winner. If he just had one offer, he would leap at the chance to leave his current job. With two good offers on the table, though, he knew that if he made the wrong choice he would never forgive himself. He wanted to ask both Gil and the city firm for more time to make a decision. He just couldn't decide how to ask for that.

His girlfriend thought he should accept Gil's offer. Rita argued that if they decided to start a family in the next couple of years, a flexible job with no commute would allow him to be home more with her and the baby. While it was nice that Rita had a clear opinion, he couldn't decide how much weight to give it. Since she turned 35, Rita had been talking about marriage and babies more and more. Miguel couldn't really think about marriage because for the past few years, he had been thinking quite a bit about breaking up with Rita. She was great, and he really loved her, but he wasn't sure if he was ready to settle down just yet. He had only had a couple of relationships before he met Rita, and always thought it might be a good idea to date around a bit more before getting married...just to give himself more options. Except, when he thought about ending things with Rita, he got really sad. She was so awesome, really, and what if he never met anyone he liked this much? On the other hand, what if he ended up regretting not dating around when he had the chance?

If he was going to stay with Rita, and maybe start a family someday, a flexible job close to home would be a definite plus. But, if he broke up with Rita, he could move into the city, which would *remove the commute problem. Also, there was more opportunity for dating in the city. If he was making more money and working for a big-shot company, he might be more attractive to women. Miguel realized that what he really needed to do was make a decision about the relationship before deciding about the job. But there was no time for that. Choose the job you want, then decide about the relationship later. Only...isn't choosing a life partner more important than some job? Miguel could not decide what to decide first!*

Analysis Paralysis: Stuck in the Hallway

With a girlfriend he loves, and two attractive job offers, Miguel seems to have acquired the basic ingredients of a good life. However, he is having trouble putting those ingredients together to make something substantial for himself. Instead of creating a structure in which to enjoy his life, Miguel has spent years at a job he doesn't like and been unable to either commit to Rita or leave that relationship to look for someone else. Like a swimmer treading water, he is struggling and putting a great deal of effort into staying in one place. As he does this, more time passes. What keeps Miguel from moving forward is the fear of making a wrong choice. Unfortunately, not making choices has its own consequences. His fear of taking a job that is not right for him has led him to spend years in the wrong job. His fear of choosing the wrong partner has kept him from building more of a life with the person he loves. Miguel avoids making choices because he can imagine a future self who regrets the decision he is about to make. To avoid becoming this future self, he puts off making a decision. The problem with not choosing is that not choosing is also a choice.

Miguel is a good guy with the best of intentions. What makes him vulnerable to this pattern of fear and avoidance has to do with the way human beings experience time. While it may not be completely obvious what the hell Miguel's problem is, you would be right to guess that sticky thoughts have something to do with it. Miguel's position, as he experiences it, is that of a person standing in a hallway trying to choose between two closed doors. Door number one is the job in the city; door number two is the local job. At other times, door number one is proposing to Rita, and door number two is breaking up with Rita. As Miguel sees it, if he chooses the right door, he will end up being happy. If he chooses the wrong door, he will not only be unhappy, but he will have to live with the bitter knowledge that he could have been happy had he only chosen the other door. It's similar to the dilemma faced by the protagonist in Frank R. Stockton's famous nineteenth-century story "The Lady, or the Tiger?" In it, a despotic king forces one of his male subjects to choose between two sealed doors. Behind one is a beautiful lady who will be his bride. Behind the other is a ferocious tiger who will devour him on the spot. Needless to say, this is not an enviable position to be in, and one can see how someone might want to put off making the decision. Miguel's situation, however, is really nothing like that.

The perception that there is a happy and an unhappy outcome behind the doors that Miguel is choosing between is actually an illusion. Much of the information about what either job option would really be like lies in the future. Since the future is largely unknowable, the outcome of choosing either job is ambiguous. The anxious mind does not like ambiguity (remember the thing in the bushes?). It wants to prepare you for the worst. While in fact, either job will probably include some good things and some bad things, in an effort to reduce the ambiguity, Miguel's anxious mind offers him the thought that one of the options is likely right and one is wrong. Because of cognitive fusion, Miguel experiences these thoughts of "rightness" and "wrongness" as more than just thoughts. When he considers the possible outcomes of his decision, Miguel's experience is that the "rightness" or "wrongness" of each door *exists* independent of his actually choosing and going through that door. As far as Miguel is concerned, the "wrong" choice is just sitting there, waiting to be chosen, like a hungry tiger. It's this illusion that leads to his fear and his desire to remain in the hallway as long as possible.

In our calmer moments, what we know to be true is that ultimate outcomes do not exist independent of a series of actions that, once taken, tend to lead to more choices. Whether a given decision ultimately turns out to be "right" or "wrong" depends not so much on the initial choosing part but on what comes next. Whatever Miguel chooses, whether or not it turns out to be the "right" choice will depend largely on his ability to embrace that choice and take subsequent action to *make* it the right choice. His power to determine the ultimate outcome of his choice goes far beyond the moment of choosing. Once he accepts a job offer, whether or not it works out will depend on things like showing up for work consistently, making an effort to connect with coworkers, asking for clear direction in his role, and putting in the time and effort to master the skills involved. In a similar way, finding happiness in his life with Rita will depend on his ability to embrace her as his life partner, taking her needs into account and communicating his own, and making plans and following through on them. Keeping his options open, on the other hand, could be the very thing that spells the end of an otherwise happy relationship.

Speaking of keeping our options open, it's not just the fear of making the wrong choice, it's the fear of losing those good options. Sticky thinking not only leads Miguel to experience the "wrong" outcome as real and wrong in an already existing, predetermined way. He experiences the "right" outcome as equally real. He imagines that if he chooses the "wrong" door, and leaves the hallway, the "right" door will no longer be available to him. He will have lost not only the right choice, but all of the good things that he believes would have followed it. This is the perceived *opportunity cost* that we referred to in chapter two. When the goal is *maximizing,* or making the best choice possible, it's not enough to know that a choice is likely to work out well for you. We want to know that there is not a better choice out there. As long as he stays in the hallway, Miguel has the comfort of knowing that he still has the possibility of choosing the right door. All those beautiful women who want to date him are still in the city, just waiting for him to move there. For some people, staying in the hallway as long as possible, hoarding their options, becomes an implicit life goal. For Miguel, this has meant avoiding a job change and remaining with, but uncommitted to, Rita. The problem with deciding not to decide is that there isn't much going on in the hallway. All of the good stuff in life happens on the other side of those doors.

Obsessive Regret

The stickiness of anxious thinking can play another trick as well, this time after we have made a choice and left the hallway. Having chosen, followed through, and arrived at an outcome, it is still impossible to say for certain whether the choice we made was in fact the best choice to make. Even if our choice has led to a happy outcome, there's no way of knowing whether another door might have been even *more* right than the one we chose. Sometimes we become convinced that the *right* choice was the one we left behind that unopened door, abandoned when we left the hallway via another route. The very thought of this can trigger intense anxiety. In our fused experience, the right choice is still there, waiting for us, like an abandoned child. We can feel an urgent need to go back, to re-choose. Our heart races and our muscles tighten. We are struggling to make a different choice, to undo what has been done, to change what is unchangeable. In these moments, the past, which we usually experience as frozen and fixed, a story that has already been written, appears to us as something subject to our influence and efforts. Our thoughts about the past, which are here, now, are fused with the reality they refer to. Our body struggles to act on the past the same way it would act on the present. This is another form of time fusion.

Our Experience of Time

In Book 11 of his *Confessions,* Saint Augustine poses the question "What is time?" He points out that time has three parts: past, present, and future. He also observes that past and future do not really exist, since we can only experience them when they are the present. Yet, we experience the *passing* of time, and we even measure it. What Augustine concludes is that this experience of the passing of time, and perhaps time itself, is the creation of our minds. He compares the problem to our experience of music. When we listen to music, we are hearing distinct sounds. What makes a sound music is its relationship to the sounds that came before and after it. If we are always in the present moment, how is it that we hear music and not just a sound? Music, according to Augustine, is possible because of the mind, which includes both memory and anticipation. Time, like music, is constructed by the mind, from our memories and anticipations. In other words, time, as we experience it, is made of thoughts.

We tend to think of and speak about time using space as a metaphor. "Measuring" the "passing" of time with the movement of a second hand around the face of a clock is an example of this spatial metaphor. We speak of "moving forward" into the future, and leaving the past "behind" us. In his witty and provocative book, *The Stuff of Thought*, psycholinguistics researcher Steven Pinker (2007) explores the various ways humans express their experience of time. He notes that, while space is universally used as a metaphor for time, exactly how it is used varies. In Chinese, the future is up and the past is down. In the Andean language Aymara, the future is described as being behind us, and it is the past that lies ahead. Pinker goes on to explain that the Aymara formulation probably reflects our experience of events in the past as being actual and knowable (like the hand in "front" of your face) and events in the future being hypothetical and unknown (as if hidden behind us, out of view).

This distinction between the accomplished "reality" of events in the past and the tentative "imaginary" nature of events in the future is expressed in yet another metaphor when we think of events in the past as frozen and fixed while events in the future are moveable and in flux. The British astrophysicist Arthur Eddington (1929) described this perceived "asymmetry" of time as what gives it a sense of one-way direction. As he conceived it, events appear to be increasingly random in one direction (the future) and less random in the other (the past). He referred to this phenomenon as "the arrow of time" and pointed out that it is vividly recognized by consciousness and is key to our causal reasoning. This perception of the past as fixed and the future being in flux is what seems to break down in our experience of time fusion, leading us to regard the future as determined and set in some cases, and the past as subject to change in others.

We've already looked at how this happens for Miguel. He experiences his future as fixed and determined, depending on the choice he makes in the present. Possibilities and hypotheticals are stories, speculations, projections. They may be based on past experience but, unlike the past, are subject to any manner of shifting and changing. For Miguel, instead of experiencing his hypothetical futures as in flux and subject to his subsequent choices, he experiences them as fixed and inevitable. Since at least one of these futures is perceived to be "wrong," and since he can't be sure which one that is, he becomes increasingly anxious and escapes that anxiety by avoiding making a decision. In some cases, this perception of the future as fixed and determined can lead to feelings of hopelessness, as when a person who is depressed believes that things will "never work out" no matter what they do. This experience of the future as fixed can happen even when we don't have a specific hypothesis. Miguel doesn't need a detailed narrative about what will make either of his job choices "wrong" to experience that a general "wrongness" lies behind one of those doors. The idea, vague though it may be, and the reality it refers to are fused. This leads to analysis paralysis, indecisiveness, and procrastination.

Time fusion in the opposite direction causes us to experience the past as somehow changeable or fixable. When we experience obsessive, ruminative regret, the memory of a past event and the actual event are fused in our experience. Since we can usually act on actual events (as opposed to remembered events), when this happens, we respond to the memory with fight-or-flight arousal and the drive to take action, literally struggling to prevent or change the event. This happens even when we "know" that the event is unpreventable and unchangeable because it has already occurred. This fused experience of the past also plays a role in struggles with acute grief and posttraumatic stress. Perhaps the most extreme example of this sort of fusion is a *flashback*, in which a person fully re-experiences a traumatic event as though it is happening in the present moment. The past, which only exists as a memory, is experienced as real, in flux, and requiring action.

Unled Lives

Sometimes time fusion involves fused thoughts of an alternate present based on different choices than those that were actually made. When this happens, the obsessive thoughts focus on "the road not taken." I once worked with a patient who, in spite of his many personal and professional successes, was obsessed with thoughts of how much better his life might have been if he had attended a different university. Having received offers from two top Ivy League schools, he agonized over his decision both before and after he made it. He spent much of his time at University A imagining how much happier he would have been at University B. Without any evidence, he assumed that his classes would have been more engaging and that he would have performed better because of it. His ruminations included elaborate fantasies about the cooler and more interesting friends he would have met there and the more attractive women he would have dated. Frustrated and depressed by these thoughts, he put less effort into his studies while at University A and was ambivalent about pursuing a social life. Cognitive fusion led him to experience the imagined professors, friends, and girlfriends at University B, as well as the life he would have led there, as quite real. This led him to experience their loss as equally real and very painful.

This line of thinking continued even after he graduated and entered the workforce. Observing the success of a coworker who had attended University B, he attributed all of her success solely to her having attended the "right" school. This perspective made it difficult for him to feel empowered or to take responsibility for the decisions he was making in the present. Having decided that all of his power to affect outcomes lay in the past, he tended to see himself as a victim of history, unable to alter the course of his life from his current position.

Even when we know that an unled life is a fantasy, it can still affect our happiness with the life we have. Sometimes, the fantasy isn't even our own. When I first moved to San Francisco in my twenties, I spent a lot of time in coffee shops and attending gallery openings. I belonged to a creative writing group and took improv classes at the local community college. Over time, I developed a small circle of friends that I thought of as creative and urban. This was also about the time I discovered *A Moveable Feast*, Ernest Hemingway's highly romanticized memoir of his time in Paris between the wars. Walking alongside Hem through the Latin Quarter, hanging out with the likes of Ezra Pound and James Joyce, driving to Lyon with Scott Fitzgerald, and enjoying a little glass of liqueur while listening to Gertrude Stein hold forth about her friendship with

Picasso, I couldn't help but feel that I just wasn't meeting the right people. My new friends were perfectly nice, but were they really all that witty? Were any of them brilliant? I couldn't escape the feeling that I somehow deserved better.

Now, of course, social media often provides the fantasy material by which we measure our actual, pallid reality. The carefully curated depictions of life that we find on Facebook or Instagram, where every sunset is golden and every meal a celebration of life, can lead us to feel bad about our own, comparably grubby existence. A recent review of the research on social media use and mental health (Keles et al. 2020) cites many studies that have found correlations between both the amount of time spent on social media and the number of platforms used and increased symptoms of depression and anxiety. People who deactivated their Facebook account for a month scored lower on measures of depression and anxiety and reported increased happiness and satisfaction with life (Alcott et al. 2020).

Sometimes we can entertain thoughts of alternate paths we might have taken in a lighter, less fused way. These ruminations can have the allure of fantasy and can put us more closely in touch with our current desires. If literature and movies are any indication, many of us are fascinated by the notion of alternate selves. The popular, if inscrutable, television series *Lost* portrayed two parallel universes in which alternative versions of the same characters followed very different paths. Novelists as wide-ranging as Dickens, Kate Atkinson, and Ian McEwan have capitalized on the theme. Then there is Woody Allen's offhand observation: "My one regret in life is that I'm not someone else."

Literary scholar Andrew Miller (2020) offers an extended meditation on the idea of the alternate self in his poetic book *On Not Being Someone Else: Tales of Our Unled Lives*. In it, he offers this eloquent description of the sense of loss that can accrue as the potential transitions into the actual:

> While growth realizes, it narrows: plural possibilities simmer down into one reality, haloed by evaporating, airborne unrealities. There's loss to be found, if you look, in the bare fact that

you've had only one past and arrived at only one present. Life is *exclusive…* Growth excludes and *hardens*. (7–8)

He goes on to caution that our unled lives are

part of this world as shadows are part of things, as memories are part of perceptions, as dreams are part of day…my imagined life makes this one seem like less. Instead of adding to the world, my unled life subtracts from it. (49)

Being Present with the Past and the Future

Living well with both memory and anticipation requires experiencing both as what they are: thoughts. The choices we have made, and the experiences that followed those choices, provide the memories from which we construct a narrative about the past. Like multiple biopics made by different directors, the slant of this narrative is subject to change depending on new experiences and our mood in the present moment. To some extent, we choose the past that we live with depending on how we construct the story of our lives. We may not be able to change the facts, but we can choose what is important and decide what it ultimately means. Using the defusion skills presented in part two of this book can make it easier to recognize the narrative nature of both the past and the future as we are telling ourselves these two types of stories.

When it comes to making choices, it can help to recognize the diminishing return of trying to maximize. The costs of lost time and increased distress that come with postponing choosing are often greater than those of making a sub-optimal choice. Barry Schwartz (2004) found that "satisficers," who use "good enough" as the guiding criterion when making choices, were happiest with their choices and least prone to regret. They also reported being happier with life in general and more optimistic about the future, and were less likely to experience depression. He recommends choosing when to choose by restricting our options when a decision is less than crucial and setting "good enough" as a criterion of success for most choices.

As for looking back, when considering what might have been behind those unchosen doors, it helps to consider all of the possibilities. When you conclude that you've chosen a "wrong" door, it helps to remember that the unchosen door could have been even more wrong, thereby making the chosen door the "right" one after all. As wonderful as University B might have been, with its brilliant professors and beautiful students, if it was also the university where you would have been hit by a bus on the way to graduation, University A might actually have been the "right" choice for you. In fact, as long as you're constructing narratives, why not assume that each of your unled lives was one of a series of bullets unknowingly dodged. The path you actually took is what brought you safely to this moment, where you still have the ability to make more choices.

It's not just unled lives and the story you tell about your actual life that are constructions. Even the main character of your story, what you usually think of as your *self*, is a construction of your mind. If that's so, then who is the author and the audience of all these stories in your head? This is the question we will turn to in the next chapter...when...and *if*... you choose to read it!

CHAPTER 5

Song of My Self

When I first talk to patients about the paradox of trying to control anxiety, walking them through the gorilla metaphor and various other metaphors for "letting go" of the struggle to control feelings or thoughts, the response I get is often some version of the following:

"I get the concept, and it makes a lot of sense to me, intellectually. The only problem is, I can't *stand* to be that anxious."

With patients struggling with Pure O, I hear something similar:

"I know these are just thoughts, but I'm afraid that if I let them be there, they'll just take over."

I've learned to listen closely to these concerns and to ask patients a lot of questions about what exactly they mean. For example, I might ask, "What will happen to you if you can't *stand* a feeling?" or, "What would it mean if the thoughts *took over?*" The answers I get usually lead to the same place. In most cases, patients are concerned that feeling certain feelings or sitting with certain thoughts will harm, damage, or change them in some fundamental way. The concern is for the *self,* and the implication is that certain thoughts and feelings can change the self. Do you remember those nutrition posters that proclaimed "You Are What You Eat"? Well, at times, anxiety can lead to the perception that "You Are What You Think."

The Rapist

Carl had always prided himself on being very respectful of women. Throughout his youth, he was known among his friends as a kind, sensitive guy. Now, as a devoted husband and the father of a teenage girl, he thought of himself as a feminist. That's exactly why he found the thoughts he was having lately so disturbing. It all started with the increased reporting in the news on the sexual harassment and assault of women. The issue was far from new, but the increased awareness and more open discussion of it was. Carl followed that discussion closely, alarmed not only by the extent of the problem, but by his own cluelessness and complacency.

It occurred to him that there may have been times in his past, when he was single, that he was insensitive to or even dismissive of a partner's ambivalence about having sex. It was so long ago that the memories were hazy. He could remember a couple of girls in college asking him to slow down, or saying they weren't ready. He knew that he had never pushed it when that happened. What he was less sure about was whether he had always gained clear consent from the women he did have sex with. He worried that, without intending to, he may have pushed a sexual encounter on someone who had mixed feelings about it. Put more bluntly, while he could not remember a specific instance, he worried that he might have committed date rape at some point.

When he heard reports about a celebrity assaulting numerous women after spiking their drinks, it occurred to him that he had probably been in a position to spike a woman's drink in the past. He had no idea what he would put in a woman's drink, or where he would have gotten it. Yet, he knew that he would have had opportunities to do so. Was it possible that he could do such a thing and then forget that he had done it? How could he know for sure that this had not happened at some point? The idea made him very anxious, and kept coming up.

This is the thought that came to him while he and his wife were having dinner with another couple at their favorite Mexican restaurant. He had always found Megan, his wife's coworker, to be somewhat attractive. Now she was sitting across from him at the table, and her margarita was inches away. Did he want to put something in it? He suddenly had an image of himself cornering a drugged Megan near the restrooms. The thought shocked and alarmed him. Where were these urges coming from? He reached over *and carefully moved Megan's drink out of his reach. When Megan gave him a questioning look, he said, "I was afraid I might knock it over." Of course, he was really afraid of much more than that.*

Protecting the Self

I have seen a number of men like Carl in my practice over the years. While the #MeToo movement has highlighted an epidemic of sexual harassment and abuse in our society, I would venture that none of it has been perpetrated by men like Carl. The anxiety that Carl feels about possibly violating or not respecting a woman's boundaries is a reflection of deeply held values. This is who Carl is, and, based on his history, who he always has been. The same self that responds with concern and alarm to these thoughts is the self that has been guiding Carl in his respectful interactions with women since his earliest interactions with them. When Carl hears about men spiking women's drinks, his alarm at such behavior prompts him to ask, *Would I ever spike a woman's drink?* Of course, the only way to formulate such a thought is to imagine one's self doing just that. If Carl heard about someone skydiving and asked himself, *Would I ever parachute out of an airplane?* that thought would involve an image of Carl jumping out of a plane. That's just how thoughts work. The problem for Carl is that cognitive fusion leads him to mistake his imaginary, thought-based "self" for his real self. The thought of spiking a woman's drink *feels* like actually doing it. Moving Megan's margarita out of his reach is an attempt to protect himself from these "dangerous" thoughts.

It's not just thoughts of harming others. We often feel the need to protect the self from a variety of uncomfortable thoughts, and from intense emotions as well. This is not so surprising. The idea that the self can be harmed or injured by our experiences is ubiquitous in our culture. Western religious traditions, in particular, which identify the self with the spirit or soul, have historically described it as subject to damage or contamination, emphasizing the need for "cleansing" the spirit or otherwise repairing the soul. Early on, the field of psychotherapy perpetuated this notion that the self can be "damaged," with structural models of the self that described it as subject to "injury" and "scarring." At times, patients have been taught to believe that early experiences altered not just what they think, feel, or believe, but *who they are* in a permanent, fundamental sense. Over time, there has been a shift in the field away from this structural thinking to a more functional model of the self. Instead of damaging us or leaving psychic scars, early experiences are seen as influencing what we *think* or *believe* about ourselves, others, or the world. Increasingly, this process is described as one of learning, rather than being shaped and formed. Unlike injuries and scars, which are part of *us*, as part of our *experience,* thoughts and beliefs can shift and change over time. Who we are is different from what we think, feel, or even believe. Still, the idea of a self that must be protected persists in the culture. Both the cultural idea and the individual experience that thoughts, feelings, and beliefs *are us* can be understood as a type of cognitive fusion. The thoughts and what they refer to (us) are experienced as the same thing.

Those discussions with patients about painful thoughts or feelings somehow harming or changing them lead us to important but potentially annoying questions. Who, exactly, is the "self" that would be harmed or changed? Is the self our thoughts and our feelings? Is it our memories? Or is it something more than that? If a feeling or a thought changes, does this change the self? This is a tricky thing to think about and to discuss, and it can begin to feel like a strictly philosophical discussion. It's actually less abstract than that. It's really just a close exploration of our actual experience. Still, it's often hard to look carefully at something we tend to take for granted. It takes patience. Let's go slowly.

Consciousness and the Conceptual Self

Part of what makes this so tricky is that it is us, here in our heads, our *self,* trying to notice and define this thing we call the self. The researcher and teacher Julian Jaynes, whose career focused on describing and understanding human consciousness, compared the search for the self to looking for darkness with a flashlight. In his strange, enchanting book on the subject, *The Origin of Consciousness in the Breakdown of the Bicameral Mind,* Jaynes (1976) begins his search with a description of consciousness as "an operation rather than a thing…" As an "operation," consciousness is like mathematics. Math takes things from one realm (the physical world) and maps them to another (the numerical). Consciousness operates in a similar way, constructing an internal "space" that is an analog for the real world. Jaynes points out that "space" in the mind, while a metaphor, is a universal experience. "We are always assuming a space behind our companion's eyes into which we are talking, similar to the space we imagine inside our own heads where we are talking from" (45). He calls this function of consciousness creating metaphorical space where none exists anatomically *spatialization*. He goes on to point out that even "things that in the physical-behavioral world do not have a spatial quality are made to have such in consciousness. Otherwise, we cannot be conscious of them" (60). One example of this is the spatial representation of time that we discussed in the last chapter. Jaynes maintains that this creation of spatial metaphors, even for abstract things, is required for any type of thought. Inside this metaphorical space of the mind, we manipulate ideas in much the same way as we manipulate objects in the material world. In other words, we sort through and organize complicated concepts like the ones in this chapter the way we move things about to organize a disorderly closet.

Most importantly, consciousness produces an analog experience of *us*, what Jaynes calls the analog "I," that inhabits and observes this constructed space and everything in it. This is the *you* that is reading these words right now, transforming them into spatialized concepts in the analog realm of your mind, and arranging them there as you would organize cereal boxes in the pantry, or cards in an index. This is not, however, the end of our search for the self. Among the spatialized ideas of consciousness encountered by the analog "I" is a representation of *ourselves* that we can *observe*. Jaynes calls this the *metaphor "me."* This is the self that we tend to think of when we think of ourselves. This is the central figure of the story of our lives. So here we have two senses of self. The analog "I" observing, thinking about, and narrating the story of the metaphor "me." In ACT, this metaphor "me" is referred to as *the conceptual self.* It is a concept, an idea, a construction, that we tend to think of as *us*.

This is the self that we are protecting when we avoid or attempt to control painful feelings or thoughts. More relevant for Carl, this is the self that we imagine doing things we do not wish to do when we think that we do not wish to do them. This self pops up all the time, doing all sorts of interesting things. For example, consider the thought of *not* killing someone. It's impossible to have the thought *I would never actually kill someone* without encountering an image of your "self" killing someone. Try it now. Close your eyes and think to yourself, *I would never actually kill someone.* Go ahead. Just try it, and pay close attention to what happens. See? There "you" are, killing someone. Interesting, right? But…is that really *you?*

Fusion and the Conceptual Self

The conceptual self is made up of *thoughts.* We can experience this sense of self as an image or as a story or narrative about who we are that includes judgments, memories, and ideas. We begin to work on this conceptual, verbal model of the self as soon as we learn to think and speak in words. It starts when people ask us questions like "Do you like doggies?" or "What's your favorite color?" We use the answers that we come up with to construct an internal model of who we are. We add in things we hear about ourselves, like "She's so smart!" or "He's a little shy," or "You're so funny." This construction of the conceptual self reaches the level of high art in pre- and early adolescence, when we decide what kind of music we like, which clothes we want to wear, and what sort of friends we want to have. By adulthood, we have usually added things like political leanings, a particular sense of humor, and our personal communication style. By then, the conceptual self also includes pretty firm beliefs about our abilities and vulnerabilities, our capacity to love and be loved, and our general worth. Often, these beliefs take the form of explicit or implicit rules: "If *that* happens, I must do *this*," "Other people should always do *this*," "*That* is completely unacceptable." Of course, these "rules" are not really rules, and they do not exist outside of the conceptual self.

Hopefully, by now, you'll recall that cognitive fusion is when thoughts and the reality they refer to are fused in our experience. Since the conceptual self is a verbal model, essentially made up of thoughts, it too, is subject to cognitive fusion. In this case, the reality that the thoughts refer to is *us*. This leads us to experience this constructed model or narrative as *us*…the actual *self*. When this happens, we can try to protect the conceptualized self as we would protect the physical self. We align ourselves with protective thoughts and feelings and follow the constructed rules about the self that seem to offer this protection. For example, remember Anthony and his sequestered jacket? When Anthony experiences his obsessive thoughts and anxiety about the jacket as *himself*, he can easily find himself saying things like "*I* don't want to wear the jacket" even though he loves the way it fits, and it's cold out. It's as though the anxious mind or the OCD is saying, "I am you. What I want is what you want." When Anthony buys into this, he leaves the jacket at home to protect his "self" from the snotty thoughts and anxious feelings associated with the jacket. It's sort of like the OCD has convinced Anthony to protect it from the snotty thoughts under the guise of protecting Anthony himself. The problem with this is that Anthony, the real Anthony, actually wants to wear the jacket. The conceptual self and the OCD are protected, but Anthony is left out shivering in the cold. When we start to look at practical choices related to how to behave, knowing the difference between a conceptual you that includes OCD's judgments and rules, and the larger you that may have values other than just avoiding anxiety, becomes much more than just a philosophical question. If Anthony is able to notice that the anxious thoughts about the jacket are not him, he can respond to them by saying something like *I'm noticing anxiety and the thought that I don't want to wear the jacket, AND… I want to wear the jacket because I like it, and it's cold out.*

The Self vs. Experience

Before we continue our discussion of the two senses of self, it may help to return to our earlier distinction between your self and your experience. Most of us have an intuitive sense of this distinction. For example, pick an object in your immediate environment to look at. It could be a chair, or a lamp, or a tree. As you carefully observe this object, ask yourself this question, and wait for an answer: Is this part of my experience?

Okay. My guess is, if you were looking carefully at the chair, tree, or lamp, you eventually arrived at the answer yes, which is correct. If you are observing something, it is part of your experience. In ACT we would call this the *content* of your experience. Now look at the object again, and consider this question: Is this chair, tree, or lamp *me?*

Don't overthink it. Just wait for the answer, and notice it.

Okay? In almost thirty years of walking people through this exercise, not one person has come back with the answer that yes, they are the chair, lamp, or tree. The answer, of course, is no.

Now...look at your hand. Either hand will do. Think about how, when you were an infant, this same hand was really small. Think about how you've seen it change over the years, without really noticing those changes. Let yourself imagine how this hand will look, if you're lucky, when you are ninety-five years old. Same hand, once tiny and soft, now bigger, eventually veined and bony. Yet it has been attached to *you* the whole time. Is this hand part of your experience?

The answer, again, is yes. The hand is part of the *content* of your experience (by the way, don't be too concerned by what is happening to your hand...it's normal for content to change over time). Now... Is this hand *you?*

Here is where I start to get different answers. Sometimes yes, sometimes, no, more often, "It depends..." or "Sort of..." Okay, how about this... Suppose (and please know that I would *never* actually do this) I were to chop off that hand and put it in a box in the trunk of my car? Would it then be true to say that *you* were in the trunk of my car?

Right. So, while you tend to *think* of your hand as *you*, and while you may be, quite literally, *attached* to this hand...it is not, in fact, *you*. It is part of your body, and while your body has changed a lot over the years, *you* are still the same person. There is a sense of continuity that you experience as *you*, independent of your continuously changing hand, face, and body. In ACT, we would say that this constant, continuously abiding part of you is the *context* for the shifting, growing, changing, temporary *content* of your hand.

One more round. Close your eyes for a moment and picture *yourself* as you are at this stage of your life. Notice how you look, what you're wearing, your posture. Imagine yourself doing something that you spend a lot of time doing…working, reading, exercising…just being *you*. Go ahead and do this for a minute or two.

Okay…is this image, as you hold it, part of your experience? Sure. Now… Is this *you*? Notice how this question gets harder to answer as the part of your experience becomes more personal and private, more *inside* than *outside*.

If you were following the directions, and picturing yourself, then it would seem the answer here is yes, this is you. However, please consider this… Who, exactly, was observing this image of you? Who chose the image? Who decided what you would be wearing, and what you would be doing?

Isn't it the person who is reading these words right now? The same person who is not in my trunk, and, hopefully, still attached to that ever-changing hand? The same person who has been there all along, watching but not watching that hand and everything else that has happened in your life? Could this watching part of you, this part that you rarely notice because it's always there, actually be you? In ACT, this patient, unobtrusive, quietly observant, hand-watching, self-imagining, thought-thinking, feeling-feeling, continuously continuing *you* that hardly ever gets noticed at all is called the *contextual self*. It corresponds roughly with Julian Jaynes's analog "I." It is the larger, more enduring self that looks out at the world from behind your eyes and looks inward at your thoughts. It's the *you* that experiences thoughts, memories, judgments, rules, and feelings like sadness, joy, and fear. This self is separate from these things, which are not *you*, but are all part of your experience. The you that you think about when you think about you, the *conceptual self*, is also a part of your experience, held and observed by the larger, more enduring, less visualizable, less trunkable, largely untouchable YOU that is the *contextual self*.

The Contextual Self

This is sort of a ruling-out approach to the contextual self. You can think of it as what's left when we subtract all the content of consciousness. Because the contextual self is so fundamental and behind the scenes, it's very hard to describe or discuss it in a straightforward, intellectual way. Metaphors and experiential exercises are more fruitful.

Steven Hayes offers a more experience-based definition when he refers to the contextual self as "you-as-perspective" (Hayes, Strosahl, and Wilson 1999), emphasizing that we contact this sense of self not as a being who can be observed but as "a locus from which observations are made." He goes on to posit that this fundamental distinction between transient, observable things (content) and this sense of an enduring locus from which things are observed (context) "forms the basis of the matter-spirit distinction that seems to have emerged in virtually all complex human cultures" (185).

The contextual self, also referred to as "self-as-context," is very much like the traditional concept of "spirit" in that it is ever-present, is enduring, and cannot be observed. Buddhism refers to it as "the ground of being," the wholeness of awareness itself. The psychologist and spiritual teacher Ram Dass (1971) compares this quietly abiding self to the blue sky. When we look up, we tend to focus on what is *in* the sky. If there are clouds there, this is what we see. The clouds are our thoughts, feelings, experiences... content. Usually, the clouds get all of the attention. What we tend to miss is the patch of blue that indicates a larger, enveloping sky, the ever-present context that surrounds and contains the clouds. This blue sky is the contextual self. If you are the sky and not the clouds, it is not so important to be in control of the clouds. The sky does not require protection from the clouds. It's big enough to contain all of them, without injury. Observing the clouds of our thoughts and feelings from the perspective of the sky can open us up to new levels of acceptance and openness to our experience. We are more in harmony with it, we struggle less, and we recognize that none of it is "us."

Walt Whitman pointed to this vastness in his long, gently flowing poem "Song of Myself" when he said, "I am large, I contain multitudes." In the same poem, he drew this distinction between content and context:

People I meet, the effect upon me of my early life or the ward and
city I live in, or the nation,

The latest dates, discoveries, inventions, societies, authors old
    and new,
My dinner, dress, associates, looks, compliments, dues,
The real or fancied indifference of some man or woman I love,
The sickness of one of my folks or of myself, or ill-doing or loss
    or lack of money, or depressions or exaltations,
Battles, the horrors of fratricidal war, the fever of doubtful news,
    the fitful events;
These come to me days and nights and go from me again,
But they are not the ME myself.

Learning to Be with the Contextual Self

One very straightforward way to create space between your self-as-context and the anxious thoughts, judgments, and rules that are often folded into the conceptual self is to take a breath, notice the anxious thoughts, and say to yourself, *That's not me.* "That" may be part of your experience, and perhaps even part of your experience of "self." But the you that is observing all of that is, by definition, not that. In his groundbreaking book *Brain Lock*, psychiatrist Jeffrey Schwartz (1997) formulated this idea in the helpful phrase "It's not me; it's my OCD." There is an image on the back of that book that I also find immensely helpful. It's a picture of a brain made with a functional MRI, which produces images of brain activity. It shows OCD at work, as elevated activation in the anxious parts of the brain. The image makes an impression on many of my patients with OCD as well. I like to point out that when we look at this image, we are observing OCD, and that it is also possible for them to observe their own OCD, when it's activated, in a similar way. If you are able to observe OCD operating in your mind, in the form of anxious thoughts, there must be more to you than those thoughts. The part of you that is able to observe the anxiety is the larger, broader, contextual you. This you is *not* anxiety. This you is not anxious. This you requires no protection from thoughts or from feelings.

Part two of this book presents a number of ways to create space between your self as context and your thoughts as content using the component skills of our LLAMP acronym. When we observe our experience from the perspective of self-as-context, we begin to look *at* our thoughts and feelings, rather than *through* them. A very basic way to do this is by labeling our thoughts and feelings. Labels can remind us that thoughts are thoughts and suggest ways of holding those thoughts. Also, inherent in the experience of labeling is a distinction between the content that is being labeled and the self that is doing the labeling. In addition to reminding us what to do or not do with a thought or feeling, the act of labeling reminds us that this content is not *us*. For Carl, this would mean being willing to notice and observe the imagined Carl, spiking Megan's drink and cornering her near the restrooms, then reminding himself, *That's not me.* Which, in fact, it is not. It's just the thought of something he very much would not want to do. This is his anxious mind helping him to live his values. Chapter six is devoted to the power of observing and *labeling* our experience.

The increased space between you and your thoughts adds a contextual, or *relational*, dimension to your experience. It is this awareness of the *relationship* between you and your thoughts that offers the opportunity for change. Relationships are not static. They can be characterized by varying degrees of conflict and struggle or harmony and peace. When we identify with the expansive, sky-like contextual self, we have the opportunity to hold our experience in a different way. We can carry judgments more lightly and make room for even painful thoughts and feelings. We can shift from struggling for control to something else. We can let go of the gorilla. Chapter seven is all about changing this relationship between self and experience by *letting go* of struggle.

Our instinct to struggle and protect ourselves from certain thoughts starts and ends with cognitive fusion. This can be the fusion of self with experience, as when we say "I *am* anxious" or "I *am* sad," equating ourselves with our experience in a fixed way. It can also be the fusion of negative thoughts with the reality they refer to, making them unacceptable to us. Both types of fusion set us up for a struggle to protect ourselves from our own thoughts. Chapter eight focuses on ways of reducing fusion and *accepting* our thoughts as thoughts. It includes a variety of strategies, including visualization and the use of humor, to help us experience our thoughts as both separate from their referents and separate from *us*. Creating this space makes it easier to accept the content of our experience without struggle.

One way of coming more closely in line with the contextual self, increasing our awareness of the contents of consciousness, and cultivating a compassionate acceptance for what we find there is by cultivating *mindfulness*. Chapter nine discusses the objectives and how-to of being more mindful, whether through meditation or just in how we go about living our daily lives.

Finally, in chapter ten, we will explore the power of connecting more clearly with a sense of your *purpose*, or values. Being more aware of your values, and what proceeding in a valued direction looks like, can help you to make choices based on those values rather than on anxiety or OCD. Clarity about the value of a given choice can make it easier for you to make room for and accept any uncomfortable thoughts and feelings that go along with that choice. Connecting with your values, which tend to be enduring and stable over time, can also give you a clearer sense of your true *self*, distinct from your thoughts and feelings, which tend to be more fleeting and temporary.

PART TWO

Making Thoughts Less Sticky

CHAPTER 6

The Alarm Is Not the Fire

In the first half of this book, we took a close look at anxiety and obsessive thinking, particularly in "Pure O" OCD, with a focus on cognitive fusion and how it can pull us into struggles with our thoughts and feelings. Having a firm grasp of the concepts presented thus far will make it easier to recognize fusion when it is happening. Being more aware of fusion when it happens is an important first step toward creating its opposite, cognitive defusion. If cognitive fusion is when our thoughts become stuck to the reality that they refer to, cognitive defusion is when those thoughts become less sticky. Still, at this point, you may be thinking something like *This is all very interesting, but when I'm struggling with obsessive thoughts, what exactly should I do?*

The next five chapters will address that question by introducing five skills that can help to tilt your relationship with obsessive thoughts away from fusion and struggle and toward defusion and acceptance. I use the word "tilt" to emphasize that this is a small move rather than an about-face. If you imagine yourself balanced between control and acceptance, like a person sitting in the center of a see-saw, these tools are about tipping you slightly toward acceptance. Like the person in the center of the see-saw, however, a slight tip in one direction or the other can lead to a bigger shift of energy in that direction. Just as a slight tip in the direction of control can be all it takes to send you tumbling down into compulsive struggles or complete avoidance, a gentle tilt in the acceptance direction can slide that energy in the direction of more purposeful, value-driven action.

Here are the five skills and a brief description of each:

Label: Observe and identify what is happening using labels that create defusion.

Let Go: Relax your struggle with your thoughts and lean in and feel your feelings.

Accept: Use defusion to accept thoughts as thoughts and narrative as narrative.

Mindfulness: Ground yourself in the present by noticing more of your experience.

Proceed with Purpose: Connect with your immediate purpose and act on your values.

You'll notice that the first letter of each skill spells the acronym LLAMP. I apologize for the extra L. You can imagine a lamp shaped like a llama. Utilizing each of these skills might involve any number of tools that help you develop and practice that skill. For example, the skill of *Accepting* your thoughts might involve using specific defusion exercises or simply saying yes to your experience. *Mindfulness* might involve meditation or just going for a mindful walk. While each of these are broad skill areas, you can also think of LLAMP as five "steps" that you can take, in the moment, when you are struggling. Walking yourself through each of the five steps, in order, is a good place to start. Later, you may use only two or three of the steps, depending on which ones you find to be most helpful and effective. You may find that you're more of a LAP or AMP person. Many of my patients eventually settle on something as streamlined as LA or AM. This works because all of the skills share common goals and overlap on a more fundamental level. Like training wheels, using LLAMP as five steps helps you to develop all five of these skill areas initially. By eventually applying the skills more flexibly, you'll notice that the steps sort of merge as defusion comes more naturally over time. In this chapter and the four that follow, I'll present specific tools and exercises to help you develop each skill or step. Chapter eleven offers examples of how the skills can be used together, based on the stories about "Pure O" OCD that you've already read, along with a structure for putting these skills to work for yourself.

Labeling

Labeling is the first and, I believe, most important of the five skills presented here. Unless you're able to notice and identify fusion when it's happening, you're unlikely to apply any of the other four skills. If you're unable to do anything else discussed here, please try to at least label your experience in some way. This step alone is likely to offer some degree of relief, and it sets the stage for a shift away from your "old plan" of struggling to control and change your thoughts or feelings. Labeling troubling thoughts and feelings has two benefits. First, it reminds you that certain thoughts and feelings are not what they appear to be. Second, the very act of labeling your experience creates space between you, the labeler (*context*), and your experience (*content*), making it clearer that these thoughts and feelings are not you. This tiny space between the thought and what it refers to and between you and the thought is the beginning of cognitive defusion.

Labeling is actually something that most of us do all the time. Whether they are sticky pieces of paper attached to objects or simply mental designations, labels help us to categorize things and suggest how we should engage with those things. Let's start with a few easy examples. I would venture to guess that in your home there are a variety of liquids stored in containers. I would also guess that there are labels on those containers indicating, at the very least, whether the liquids inside fall into the category of "beverages" or "cleaning products." These labels guide you in which liquids to drink and which ones to clean with. Pretty helpful, right? More often, the labels are not physical objects, but classifications you hold in your mind. Your labels for the people you encounter probably includes designations like "boss," "lover," "friend," "acquaintance," and "stranger." The label you apply guides your choices in how to engage with a specific person. Over time, you may consciously change these labels as a way of reminding yourself to hold or regard a person in a different way.

This happens when we come to view a former acquaintance as a "friend," or a former friend as "not a friend."

Labeling Feelings

Labeling strong emotions can help us shift our perspective away from looking at the world *through* those emotions to looking *at* the emotions themselves. This gives us more room to maneuver, opening us up to more options of how to respond. Labeling and looking at emotions also helps us move from the fused experience of "I *am* sad" or "I *am* afraid" to the more defused awareness that "I'm feeling sadness" or "I'm experiencing some fear." Stepping back from feelings enough to label them can be challenging, especially when it comes to feelings of intense anxiety. One reason for this is that anxiety often presents itself as something other than what it really is. Anxiety is basically an alarm that goes off both in our body and in our mind to alert us to a possible danger or threat. Like most alarms, anxiety is very unpleasant. This helps to assure that it gets our attention. More importantly, as with any alarm, anxiety is sometimes triggered when there is no actual threat, and can continue even after the threat has been addressed. It's sort of like having a very sensitive smoke detector that's hardwired into your home. You can't disconnect it, and sometimes it goes off when you're just making toast. Now, it probably isn't a good idea to call the fire department every time the alarm goes off. Instead, it's helpful to treat the alarm as information and to seek more information before deciding whether to take further action. For example, do you smell smoke? Do you see flames?

But what happens if you mistake the alarm for the fire? What if, in your experience, the alarm and the fire are essentially the same thing? Cognitive fusion can lead us to respond to the alarm as though it were the fire itself. Instead of checking for smoke or flames, we respond to the sound of the alarm by running outside, rolling on the ground, and screaming for the fire department. Over time, we may even forget that there's any difference between an alarm and a fire, regularly spraying the alarm, ourselves, and everything in sight with the fire extinguisher. This is where labeling can be extremely helpful. Observing our physical feelings of anxiety and labeling them as "sensations," for example, can help us make room for them and experience them as separate from the story they are trying to tell. Other useful labels for the experience of anxiety might be "alarm bells ringing" or "my engine revving." These labels can remind us that anxiety itself, while unpleasant (like those piercing beeps), is not actually dangerous. It can make it easier for us to let go of our struggle to control or get rid of the anxiety, giving us more options for what we choose to do next.

Over the years, I've noticed that my most anxious patients tend to have very colorful and impressionistic ways of thinking and talking about their experience of anxiety. For example, they may describe anxiety with phrases like "I'm crawling out of my skin," "My head is going to explode," or "I'm going to die." These thoughts are all referring to sensations they are experiencing. A more accurate labeling of these sensations might be "I feel my skin tingling," "There's a pressure in my head," and "My heart is racing." These labels highlight and describe the alarm that is going off in your body, rather than telling a story about a nonexistent fire. The problem with the more colorful, fire-like thoughts is that they tend to set off more alarms.

Labeling Thoughts

You have thoughts all day long. A lot of these thoughts are very helpful. For example, buying into and following thoughts like *It's almost time for lunch, I should call my sister,* or *I need to pee* will help you to eat regularly, connect with loved ones, and avoid unpleasant accidents. Not all of our thoughts are equally helpful, however. If we've gone over a thought countless times, if the thought refers to events beyond our control, or if it is distorted and biased, it is often of little use to us. Labeling an obsessive, anxious thought as "not helpful," "not realistic," or "too much" can put us on alert to treat this thought differently from other, more helpful thoughts. When we label a particular thought or line of thinking as "obsessive" or "OCD," this tips us off that we may want to engage with this thought in a different way. Which label will be most helpful for you depends on your specific situation and is worth a little thought.

One way to remind ourselves that anxious thoughts are not exactly what they appear to be is to label them in a way that highlights their inherent bias. You might remember our discussion of *threat bias* in chapter one. This is when the anxious mind, to protect us, leans toward presenting things as worse than they actually are. It can be helpful to keep in mind that the anxious part of the brain is highly specialized. Being anxious is its job. It's the only thing it knows how to do. It's a bit like the outraged "shock jocks" you sometimes hear on talk radio. Expressing outrage and consternation is their business. What you're hearing is not exactly an objective reporting of events in the world. There's an angle there. The same is true in advertising. When you know that someone is trying to sell you a product or a service, you're probably more careful about accepting their statements at face value. In this case, the shock jock or ad agency is the anxious part of your brain. Labels for anxious thoughts that capture their inherent bias might include "spin," "marketing," or "hype."

When Anthony and I worked together on his obsessive disgust and compulsive avoidance of his new jacket, he chose "propaganda" as a label for all the anxiety-biased thoughts and associations that came up when he thought about, looked at, touched, and eventually started to wear the jacket. You'll recall that Anthony's thoughts were focused on "old guy snot." Since he knew that snot was not especially dangerous, Anthony was able to recognize his thoughts about it as judgmental, somewhat arbitrary, and markedly biased. When he noticed these thoughts coming up, he began to label them as part of an ongoing anti-snot "smear campaign" by the anxious, obsessive part of his mind. To bring the point home, when the thoughts persisted, he intentionally pictured them as angry picketers holding signs that said things like "Gross!" "Snot Sucks!" and "*SNOT* in my backyard!" This made it easier for him to notice the thoughts without embracing or identifying with them. Imagining the thoughts in this way helped him to see that they had their own agenda, which differed in many ways from his. Anthony realized that, from a values perspective, he was actually fairly neutral or at least moderate in his views on snot. At the very least, he was able to identify that snot was not as important to him as his obsessive thoughts would indicate. Labeling his thoughts as unfair "snot shaming" made it even easier for him to simply observe these biased thoughts, allowing his obsessive mind to have its own opinion without buying into it himself.

Sophie also used labeling to effectively create distance between herself and her anxious questions about whether or not she "really" loved her parents. She often described these obsessive thoughts as "oppressive" and the questioning nature of the thoughts as feeling like an "interrogation." Based on this, she came up with the label "The Love Police" to describe the squad of obsessive thoughts that routinely showed up to harass her. This label played into Sophie's anti-authoritarian streak in a helpful way. When Sophie thought of these challenging questions as coming from "The Love Police," she was able to sidestep defending herself in favor of ignoring or dismissing the thoughts. While she initially thought of "The Love Police" as threatening, she eventually came to see them as "Keystone Cops," responding to them with an eyeroll and what she eventually identified as her most powerful label, "*What*ever!"

Having a Thought vs. Buying a Thought

It's important to notice that labeling a thought is not the same as changing or getting rid of the thought. We still have the thought. The label just prompts us to interact with it in a different way. In ACT, this is often referred to as the difference between *having* a thought and *buying* the thought.

Sushi Boats

Have you ever been to one of those sushi places where you sit at the bar and these little boats float by with pieces of sushi on board? If you haven't, it's worth looking into. Food doesn't get much more fun than this. When you see a piece of sushi you like, you take it off the little boat and put it on your plate. What I like about this arrangement is that if something looks suspicious or unappealing to me, I can just let it float by. These little food-laden boats floating past my plate remind me of the stream of consciousness. All day long, thoughts float by. Most are unremarkable, some are helpful and appealing, and some are suspect or downright disturbing. *Having* our thoughts is like having the boats of sushi float past. *Buying* a thought is more like taking a piece of sushi, putting it on our plate, and eating it. The important thing to keep in mind at one of these sushi bars is that you don't have to eat every piece of sushi that comes by. If you did, it would probably be a lot less fun. Labeling thoughts as "not helpful," "too much," or "questionable" can make it easier to let them just float by. This is not the same as changing or not having the thought. It's there, right in front of us, like it or not. We're just deciding not to put it on our plate and eat it. Sometimes, a thought finds its way onto our plate before we notice it. Sometimes, we've already taken a bite before realizing what's going on. The nice thing about the stream-of-consciousness sushi bar is that here, you're allowed to put that half-eaten piece of sushi onto the next little boat that comes past and let it float away. Just don't try that at an *actual* sushi bar!

Junk Mail

Obsessive thoughts in particular can be a lot like junk mail or spam originating from the anxious part of your brain. The thing about junk mail is that, over time, it becomes pretty easy to recognize it. One reason is that we tend to get the same or similar junk mail over and over again. You start to recognize the pattern right from the start: "You may have already won a...," "Don't miss this great opportunity to...," "Dear Sir/Miss, I am an exiled crown prince reaching out to you as a trustworthy person of trust..." After a while, we don't really feel a need to read the whole thing. We send it straight to the recycle bin. What allows us to do this so efficiently is that we've developed a clear category of correspondence that we label as "junk." In some ways, the thoughts that come into your mind are not so different from mail showing up in your mailbox or email inbox. While I'm sure that most thoughts you have are very important, and at times even profound, is it possible that some of your thoughts are just...well...junk? This is not intended as an insult, and it certainly isn't personal. Remember that anxiety is a blunt instrument, and the anxious part of the brain is not exactly the *smart* part of the brain. For all of us, it tends to send a lot of messages that we can afford to disregard. We can use the smart part of the brain to identify these superfluous messages, in part because they tend to focus on topics we've already covered exhaustively. Once we've recognized a pattern, we can label thoughts that match it as "junk mail." At first, this means not spending so much time poring over the fine print. Eventually, it means not even opening the message. Notice, this is not about stopping the junk mail from coming to your mailbox. It's about what you do with it once it's there. You can't unsubscribe from your anxious mind. It's impossible to stop yourself from *having* a thought. But maybe you don't have to *buy* it.

"Extra" Anxiety

What's tricky about anxious thoughts is that, even when they're extreme or repetitive, they're not necessarily completely wrong. Sometimes even junk mail can actually make a good point. This was the problem with Lou's anxious thoughts about his relationship with his young son. The fact is, relationships do shift and change over time, and it's hard to know how things will unfold, even between a father and son who are very close. Lou loved his son and hoped they would stay close. Being concerned about that and attentive to it was not a bad thing. With anxiety, as with so many things, it's a matter of degree.

Suppose you want to cross a busy street. Having some anxiety about this proposition keeps you from running out into the path of a speeding vehicle. You want to have enough anxiety about crossing the street to prompt you to cross at the light, wait for traffic to stop, and look both ways. This much anxiety actually *helps you* to cross the street. If you have so much anxiety about crossing the street that you wait through multiple cycles of the light, step off the curb only to leap back onto it in terror, and eventually decide that you really don't want to cross the street at all, you probably have more anxiety than you need. The anxiety that you experience over and above the anxiety that helps you cross the street safely is *extra* anxiety. Life often gives us more of something than we actually need, whether it's food, companionship, time, work, or streaming options. It can be helpful to designate the superfluous part of what's offered to us as "extra." This reminds you that you don't need to eat all of that extra large portion of fries, accept every holiday party invitation, or watch every new television series you hear about. There's great value in being able to say, "Thanks, but I'm good."

Some of Lou's anxiety about his relationship with his son helped him attend to and care for that relationship. To the extent that it moved him to get away from work at a decent time, make plans to hang out with his son on the weekends, and be attentive and present when he and Adam were together, the anxiety was doing its job. The problem was the *extra* anxiety. When the anxiety worked overtime, it sent Lou upsetting messages about the future. To avoid these, Lou ended up avoiding coming home early, spent less time with Adam on the weekends, and became increasingly absorbed in his own anxious thoughts. As with the person trapped on one side of a busy street, instead of helping Lou to get what he wanted, all the *extra* anxiety thwarted him, separating him from his son. Over time, Lou was able to draw a line between the level of concern that helped him attend to his relationship with Adam and all the *extra* anxiety that was unhelpful. Now he still *felt* all of the anxiety, but he tried to base his *choices* on the helpful anxiety and on his values. Labeling helped with that.

A few years ago, my partner and I remodeled the unfinished basement of our home, turning it into a combination laundry/rumpus room. This meant that our old hot water tank, which previously sat on a concrete slab that sloped toward a drain, ended up on top of a brand-new hardwood floor. I was very happy with how the room turned out, especially the floors. Suddenly the hot water heater that I had never given a second thought became a source of worry and concern. What if it sprung a leak? I had heard of water tanks failing and completely flooding homes. I started googling things like "How do you know if your water heater is failing?" I noticed the urge to "check on" the water heater at random times, and when we went out of town, I considered turning off the water supply. I recognized this as GAD pushing into the OCD zone and managed to resist most of these urges. Then I learned about what I judged to be a reasonable precaution: an emergency shut-off valve. It involved installing a pan under the water heater that held a water sensor. The sensor was connected to a shut-off valve at the top of the tank. If there was a leak that wet the sensor in the pan, the water supply would be automatically shut off. I had one installed immediately. What surprised me, however, was that the thoughts about flooding and damaged floors continued to come. I thought of ways that the shut-off valve could fail to work, and other things that could go wrong. When I finally took a close look at what was going on, I realized that the shut-off valve was as far as I was willing to go to protect my new floors. The inconvenience of checking on the water tank or taking any other precautions far outweighed the small risk of failure that remained. In other words, I decided that I had done all that I could reasonably do. The continuing anxiety and thoughts about the hot water heater were all "extra." It reminded me of those notices you get to renew your subscription to a magazine even though you've already paid for the next two years. Once I made this determination, I began to label these feelings and thoughts as "extra." When they showed up, I thanked my mind for looking out for my floors and noted that since I had done all I was willing to do, none of these thoughts were actionable. The thoughts didn't stop right away, but they concerned me much less.

One more note about extra anxiety. Most of us really don't want it. That's understandable. However, struggling to stop your brain and your body from giving you extra anxiety is not likely to work. It's important to remember that all of this largesse is coming from the part of your brain whose mission is to protect you at all costs. As we covered in chapter one, if you refuse or push back against what is essentially a warning, it will likely become more insistent. Rather than trying to "change your mind," it might make more sense to graciously thank your mind for offering you all this extra protection. It's not unlike sidestepping a struggle with the server who brings you that ginormous serving of fries. Just say, "Thanks." You don't have to eat them all.

Inside vs. Outside

One very straightforward way to draw a clearer distinction between the internal, thought representation of a thing or event and the external, real thing or event is by labeling one "inside" and the other "outside." Remember the example in chapter three of the *inside* goat being attacked by a wolf while the *outside* goat was sleeping peacefully in the meadow? Labeling which goat is which is a simple way to highlight that they are two different things. Anthony used this pair of labels to help distinguish his jacket from his judgments about it. When Anthony closed his eyes and recalled the sneezing incident, focusing on his feelings of disgust, it was easy for him to see his jacket as covered in snot. When he opened his eyes and looked at the real jacket, it appeared to be clean. Using the inside/outside labels made it clearer to Anthony that there were two jackets. I suggested that he not wear the snotty inside jacket but experiment with wearing the outside jacket. Eventually, he was able to report, "The inside jacket is still disgusting to me, but the outside jacket seems to be okay."

A similar distinction helped Lou to feel less triggered by thoughts of his son growing distant from him. When he allowed himself to pay attention to these thoughts, one of the first things he noticed was that the *inside* Adam was anywhere from fourteen to twenty years old, depending on the day and the specific thoughts he was having. *Outside* Adam was consistently eight years old. Similarly, while *inside* Adam wasn't very interested in hanging out, *outside* Adam usually wanted nothing more than to spend time with his dad. Formulating his experience in this way made it possible for Lou to make a clearer distinction between the imagined Adam and the real one. This in turn begged the question: Which Adam was more important to Lou?

"Not Me"

Finally, labeling can also help to decrease the fusion of your self with your experience. A relatively direct way to create space between yourself and sticky thoughts and feelings is to label them as "not me." This was what Carl eventually learned to do when he had anxious thoughts about harming women. This label can be useful with any sort of anxious thoughts, even if they don't involve a specific reference to the self. First, allow yourself to focus on and attend to the unpleasant thoughts and feelings. Closing your eyes can help you to get a clear sense of the ideas, images, emotions, and physical sensations that you're struggling with. You might also notice judgments you have about your experience. Then, observing all of this, gently remind yourself that "this is not me." *You* have been here all along, and will continue to be here. *This* is your experience at the moment, and it is subject to change. The space this label creates between you as context and everything else as content can make it easier to let go of the struggle to change or control your experience, which you might recognize as step two. In the next chapter we will look more closely at what this struggle entails and exactly how to begin to let go of it.

CHAPTER 7

The Opposite of Struggling

When you experience your thoughts and feelings and yourself as the same thing, change is very difficult. It's like living in one-dimensional space. You and your experience are all contained in one continuous, straight line. Here, change means changing your experience. One way we try to do this is through our behavior: avoidance, checking, rituals, eating, shopping, substance abuse. This adds a second dimension. In this two-dimensional way of living, the horizon is the continuous line of self-fused-with-experience, and our behavior is an up-or-down attempt to escape from that line. However, because compulsive behavior is driven by the very thoughts and feelings that we are trying to escape, any change it offers is only temporary. Checking, rechecking, straightening, ordering, seeking reassurance, or avoiding all serve the agenda of your anxious thoughts and feelings. Adopting them as *your* agenda reinforces the notion that you and your anxiety are the same thing. Whether movement is up or down, it's still defined in terms of the continuous line of experience. When you're lost in that experience, your choices are its choices.

Letting Go

Learning to notice yourself as *separate* from your experience introduces a third dimension: *relationship*. It is in this relational dimension that a completely different order of change can occur. How do you, as the context, *relate* to your experience, the content? How do you encounter, hold, and interact with your thoughts and feelings? Change is no longer limited to changing your experience. Even if your thoughts and feelings remain the same, the *relationship* between you and that content can change. Instead of choices being limited to up-or-down responses to your experience, choices can be made by the self, based on something more enduring than thoughts and feelings. The flatness of the two-dimensional world opens up to a more expansive, three-dimensional space, offering more flexibility and freedom to choose. This chapter is about creating change within that third, relational dimension. When your body is tense and you are focused on controlling or changing your thoughts or feelings, your relationship to that content is one of struggling. This chapter is all about tilting toward the opposite of struggling by *letting go*.

This brings us back to that gorilla metaphor from chapter one. Imagining your anxiety as a gorilla, or a monster, or even a particularly unpleasant person can help you focus on the nature of your relationship with your anxiety. Like anxious thoughts and feelings, the gorilla shows up at your door unexpectedly. Like anxiety, the gorilla is imposing and unpleasant. Since you can't leave the room (in this metaphor, you *are* the room), it's not surprising to find yourself struggling to force the gorilla out of the room. In the introduction, we went over not only why this is unlikely to work, but also how it makes things worse. Since this gorilla is actually made of struggle and control, those responses make the gorilla bigger and stronger. If we look closer, this metaphor can increase our awareness of four important things about your relationship with anxiety. First, imagining your anxious thoughts and feelings as a gorilla can help you recognize that, like you and the gorilla, you and your anxiety are two distinct entities. Second, it can help you notice that you're *struggling* to control or get rid of your anxiety. Third, this metaphor can prompt you to consider how this relationship could be different: Is there another way to be in a room with a gorilla? Finally, it suggests a specific way to accomplish this change in the relationship. The opposite of holding onto a gorilla is letting go.

Letting Go with Your Body

Because anxiety is a very physical response, one way of noticing how you are relating to your experience is to pay attention to how your *body* is responding to your thoughts and feelings. When you focus on your anxious thoughts and feelings, are you aware of tension in your body?

This tension is part of the relationship between you and the thoughts and feelings. It's the observable part of you holding onto or struggling with the gorilla. Noticing this tension can help you to recognize and then shift this relationship from one of struggling to the opposite of that. This shift can happen even if the tension doesn't change. It's not necessarily about relaxing your muscles, though that can help. It's more about acknowledging your ongoing struggle against or resistance to your experience, and tilting your intent away from that struggle. This is *letting go*.

While the amount of energy it frees up can be significant, letting go itself is a small and subtle shift. It's both instantaneous and ongoing. Letting go is rarely something we do once and we're done. We may let go tentatively at first, or only for a fleeting moment. Almost as soon as we notice we have let go, we may notice that we are holding on again. That's okay, because we can let go over and over again, for as long as necessary. Letting go is a choice. We make that choice in an instant. However, since struggling is such a well-rehearsed habit for most of us, we may have to keep making that choice.

Try It Now...

Rather than thinking about it too much, it might help to just try letting go now. Think of a recurring obsessive thought, or anything in your life that's unsettled or uncertain. It can be something small or something large, but should be something you're at least a little concerned about. After you read this paragraph, close your eyes and focus on this obsession or unsettled thing. Notice how it appears in your awareness, both the thoughts and the emotions related to it. The thoughts may include images or a sort of unfolding story. The emotions may register more in specific parts of your body, or they may be more diffuse. Sit with this for a moment, then see if you can notice any resistance or tension between yourself and these thoughts and feelings. Pick a spot in your body where you are most aware of this resistance or tension. Take a deep breath and hold it. As you hold your breath, focus on that spot, feeling the tension between you and your experience. As you slowly exhale, imagine relaxing that tension slightly. Just as letting go of an object does not require completely opening your hands, just relaxing your grip a little, letting go of an obsessive or unsettling thought requires just a gentle release. Sit for a bit and notice what it feels like to be less resistant and to struggle less against these thoughts and feelings. If you notice that you are still struggling, take another deep breath, focusing on the spot where you feel the struggle, and once again exhale slowly while thinking, *Let go.* You may need to do this several times before you sense a shift. Try it now.

Remember, the goal is not to get rid of the thoughts and feelings you've been resisting. They will still be there. This is about a small shift in your relationship to your experience. When you're not struggling as much with these thoughts and feelings, you'll begin to notice more space between you and them. Your relationship to them will be "looser." It will include more "air." Things may quiet down a little. If not, they may be noisy in a way that's less problematic. In the moments after letting go, you might notice your breathing or your heart beating, like the tentative quiet that appears when a physical struggle suddenly stops. It's not exactly a relaxing feeling. There may be an expectant sense of "what happens next?" Resist the temptation to seek an answer to that question. Just sit for a moment with the experience of having let go, even just a little.

If you have trouble finding tension or resistance in your body, or if it's hard to imagine letting go of it, you can intentionally choose to locate that tension in your hands. We use our hands to manipulate and control all sorts of things. They are an obvious place to localize your experience of resistance and struggle. While you are noticing troublesome thoughts and feelings, slowly make two fists. Allow your fists to tighten until you can feel the tension between you and your experience there. As you breathe in, imagine that you are using your fists to contain, control, or resist the unsettled or painful thoughts and feelings. As you hold your breath, notice what this resistance feels like, not just in your fists but in your whole body. As you slowly exhale, gradually relax your fists, eventually opening your hands and allowing them to rest palms up. As you do this, think, *Let go.*

If you have trouble pinning down what the problematic thoughts or feelings are, just try visualizing a gorilla. Let the gorilla stand in for your obsessions and all that is unsettled, unruly, and unpredictable in your life.

When you clench your fists, imagine that you're holding onto the fur of this big, threatening gorilla. Feel the tightness and control that your fists represent. Notice the push against all that the gorilla represents. Then, as you exhale, imagine letting go of the gorilla. Because this is really a small, subtle move, the shift in the relationship may be subtle as well. With practice, it may be less so.

Be careful not to buy into thoughts about doing this "right"; let go of your judgments as well. There are countless ways to create change in a relationship. This is about finding moves that work for *you*. Feel free to experiment a bit. Letting go may be very different from what you're used to doing, so it will take some practice. Be patient with yourself.

But It's Still There

The thing about letting go is that, while it changes your relationship with the gorilla, it doesn't make the gorilla go away. Once you let go of the gorilla, it will still be there...and you will still not like having the gorilla in the room. Letting go does not change our experience any more or any less than struggling does. It only changes our relationship to that experience. Letting go may mean relaxing your muscles, but it may also mean accepting that they are tense. Anxiety is not pleasant. Fear pushes for a response. The gorilla will continue to look, act, and smell like a gorilla. It may knock over some of the furniture. It might even make a smelly mess on the rug. Being in the room with a gorilla isn't fun; however, it's not as bad as wrestling with one. Nobody is suggesting that you'll like the anxiety just because you're not struggling to get rid of it. What has changed is your relationship to it. What has left the room is the struggle.

The Mechanics of Letting Go

Thinking about and visualizing letting go is important because it reminds us that we're not trying to change the thing that we're holding on to, only our relationship to it. The body, however, has a long history of holding on. The tension you feel when you notice your resistance and struggle against certain thoughts and feelings is the fight-or-flight response. It developed over millennia to help us survive in the world. This physical tension is only helpful, however, when we're struggling against a physical threat. When we respond to obsessive thoughts this way, the tension only serves to intensify our experience of those thoughts. The fight-or-flight response is governed by the body's *sympathetic nervous system*. This is one of two control systems that regulate bodily functions from head to toe, including heart rate, respiration, digestion, muscle tension, and all of the other responses described in chapter one under the heading "Fight-or-Flight Below the Neck."

Our body has another nervous system, however, that runs parallel to the sympathetic nervous system and counteracts it in many ways. This is the *parasympathetic nervous system*. It governs the body's *relaxation response*, which allows us to recover from the fight-or-flight response. Learning to trigger the parasympathetic nervous system and encourage your body's relaxation response can help with this second step of letting go of your struggle to control thoughts and feelings. Like fight-or-flight, the body's relaxation response is largely automatic. You cannot consciously lower your heart rate or reduce your blood pressure. This is not about directly controlling or shutting down your body's automatic responses. There are small things you can do, however, to tilt your body's response gently in the direction of relaxation and letting go.

Breathing and the Vagus Nerve

Our body comes equipped with a sort of "on switch" for the relaxation response. The *vagus nerve* has wide-ranging parasympathetic functions. "Vagus" is Latin for "wandering," reflecting the nerve's far-reaching influence within the body. It originates near the base of the brain, connecting to the esophagus, the cardiac and pulmonary networks of nerves, and the smooth muscles and glands in the abdomen. Here it affects parasympathetic activity in the stomach, pancreas, liver, kidney, gall bladder, and all the way down to the colon. Stimulating the vagus nerve can trigger a pervasive relaxation response throughout the body. Fortunately for us, the vagus nerve runs right through the diaphragm, which is the stretchy, parachute-shaped muscle that separates your chest cavity from your abdominal cavity. By learning to stretch and hold your diaphragm when you inhale, you can stimulate the vagus nerve, indirectly influencing your body's relaxation response.

Even if you've never set foot in a yoga class, you already know how to stretch your diaphragm, and do so automatically when you sigh or yawn. Let's say you're late for an appointment and can't find your car keys. As you race around looking for them, your fight-or-flight response kicks in. When this happens, you tend to tighten your diaphragm, which forces you to breathe higher in your chest. This gets more air into your bloodstream, to bring oxygen to your muscles in case you need to run. Those muscles get tighter, and your heart rate and blood pressure increase. When you find your keys, the first thing you do is sigh. Sighing includes a deep breath in that stretches the diaphragm. This is followed by a brief pause, where we hold the diaphragm in this stretched, extended position. This puts pressure on the vagus nerve, switching "on" the parasympathetic nervous system and our relaxation response. When we exhale, relieving pressure on the vagus nerve, it causes our heart rate to slow down and our blood pressure to drop. The long exhale of the sigh helps keep you from getting hyperventilated from all the extra breathing you were doing while looking for your keys. Something similar happens at the end of a long day when we start to yawn. In a way, a yawn is just a long, gentle stretch of the diaphragm and a holding of that stretch, followed by an open-mouthed exhale. The holding part of the yawn stimulates the vagus nerve, making us more relaxed. One yawn usually leads to more yawning as the body prepares itself for sleep. One of the best ways to learn diaphragmatic breathing is to start by sighing or yawning and observing what happens to your diaphragm. The breathing parts of most relaxation techniques are really just stylized versions of a sigh or a yawn.

The Calming Breath

We've all been advised at one point or another to "take a deep breath" to help us calm down. What's usually missing from this sage advice is exactly how to take that deep breath. For many years, I worked with medical residents at a local teaching hospital. All of the residents I taught had spent many hours in emergency rooms, often encountering patients who were in the midst of a panic attack. Instructing these patients to take deep breaths was usually step number one. I liked to ask residents to demonstrate this for me, to show me how they would model "taking a deep breath" for a hyperventilating patient. At least half the time, they showed me a shallow, open-mouthed breath, high in the chest. Just the sort of breathing that leads to hyperventilation. Now, when it comes to anxiety and stress, medical residents are hardly representative of the population at large. They probably lean a bit more toward the "high idle" or "Type A" end of the spectrum, and they tend to be pretty invested in having the right answer to questions that come up in a seminar. All of this likely affected their breathing when I put them on the spot. What they were forgetting is something that most of them already knew, which is that there are two different muscle groups we can use for breathing, and two very different ways to breathe.

When we're engaged in aerobic activity like jogging, biking, or running from a predator, it's natural to breathe primarily by using our chest muscles. This "shallow" breathing results in the chest rising and falling. It causes more oxygen to enter the blood stream, feeding the large muscles of the arms and legs so we can fight and fly harder and faster. If we breathe this way when we're not engaged in strenuous activity, the extra oxygen can build up in the blood, causing us to eventually become "hyperventilated." There's a tipping point at which too much oxygen in the blood can itself be a trigger for a fight-or-flight response. This feedback loop is often what causes panic attacks. In contrast, "normal," non-aerobic breathing is mostly governed by the use of the diaphragm, which is below the chest. This is the way most children breathe. Somewhere along the way, a subset of people begin to breathe with their chests much of the time. Their diaphragms become less stretchy, and the muscles used for chest breathing become overdeveloped. Like medical residents, these people tend to run at a "higher idle" and are more vulnerable to acute anxiety and stress.

A good way to assess how you breathe is to sit in front of a large mirror. Place one hand high on your chest, just below your collar bone. Lay your other hand flat on your belly, right over your belly button. Relax your shoulders, then take a slow, deep breath in, watching both of your hands. Which hand moves the most when you breathe in? You may need to repeat this a couple of times. If most of the movement you observe is of the top hand, you likely have a tendency to "overbreathe," using your chest muscles. Odds are, this becomes more exaggerated during moments of intense stress or anxiety, like when your obsessive thoughts are triggered. Breathing high in your chest in this way can stimulate a stronger fight-or-flight response, leading to more struggling with your thoughts and more obsessing.

As long as you're in front of the mirror, try taking a slow, deep breath using your diaphragm. Keep the hand on your belly, and breathe in slowly through your nose. Imagine that there is a balloon in your belly, and that you are inflating the balloon as you breathe in. When the balloon is fully inflated, at the "top" of the breath, hold your breath for a few seconds. This holding move places pressure on the vagus nerve. Now exhale slowly through your mouth, like a long, relieved sigh. Repeat this two more times for a total of three cycles. This is what I like to call "the calming breath." You can use this breathing exercise whenever you notice that you're struggling with obsessive thoughts to remind you to let go of this struggle.

Some people have trouble isolating their breath in the abdomen. Despite their best efforts, the chest muscles continue to get involved in each breath in. If you find this to be the case, it might help to start by practicing the calming breath while lying flat on your back. When you lie on the floor on your back, the weight of the torso is no longer bearing down on the diaphragm, making it easier to expand it with each breath in. Also, gravity makes it harder to use the chest muscles for breathing when you are lying flat on your back. You may want to pile a few throw pillows on your belly so that you can observe how much your diaphragm is moving with each breath in. Lying on your back, breathe deeply into your belly, watching the pillows rise. At the top of the breath, hold your breath for a few seconds, then exhale in a long, relaxing sigh, letting the pillows go down with your belly. Pause again at the bottom of the breath, then repeat the exercise. If you like, you can do this for ten minutes or so every night at bedtime. Regular practice helps you to master proper form for belly breathing and stretches and strengthens the diaphragm, making it easier to take calming breaths while sitting or standing when you're triggered throughout the day. If you'd like to become more proactive about belly breathing, try putting little stickers around where you'll see them during the day. Put one on your phone, on the fridge, in your car. When you see a sticker, take one deep belly breath in, hold it for a moment, then exhale long and slow.

Leaning In

Letting go can be tentative. It can feel like you're just waiting to grab hold again. To shift more fully out of struggling, it can help to actively *lean in* to your experience, focusing on the thoughts and opening yourself up to feeling what is there to be felt. I think of "leaning in" as taking letting go to the next level. Once you have relaxed your struggle to control or get rid of anxious thoughts and feelings, see if you can go a little further and allow yourself to settle gently into those thoughts and feelings.

If you have much experience driving on icy roads, you know that when you hit a patch of ice, the car may start to skid to the left or right. The instinctual response to this temporary loss of control is to slam on the brakes and turn the steering wheel away from the direction the car is sliding in. Ordinarily, this response would increase your control over the car's movement. On ice, however, this can easily lead to a complete loss of control, causing the car to spin. Instead, tapping the brakes only lightly and turning *into* the direction of the spin is more likely to get the car safely to the other side of the ice. I think this is a great example of how the effort to control something can lead to a loss of control. It's the momentary acceptance of being out of control, the *leaning in*, that allows us to get safely across the ice. Letting go and leaning into feelings of anxiety can feel like the wrong thing to do. Letting go of control and feeling what is there to be felt, however, can allow us to make choices that work for us in the long run.

Another metaphor I like for leaning in has to do with downhill skiing. If you have ever skied down a mountain with any success, you have likely learned that the way to keep from falling down is to *lean in* to the slope of the mountain. This is counterintuitive, since our instinct is to lean away from the direction our feet are sliding in. However, if we can let go of that impulse and lean forward, we are more likely to remain upright.

My one attempt at downhill skiing was too sad and embarrassing to be of use here. Instead, I have a story about letting go and leaning in that involves *simulated* skiing. I was in my early twenties and visiting the Louisiana State Fair with my family. One of the most talked-about attractions at the fair was a simulated downhill skiing "experience." It was essentially a tiny box-like movie theater situated atop a foundation of hydraulic lifts and springs that could rock and shake the theater and tilt it at odd angles. It probably seated about twenty people. My brother and I scored seats in the front row, while my parents ended up in the last row, at the very back. The fifteen-minute movie was a montage of rapid slalom skiing and daring ski jumps filmed from the skiers' perspective. The theater leaned left and right in synchrony with the tilting of the camera on the slalom runs, and tilted dramatically forward when skiers raced down a jumping ramp, somehow giving us the stomach-churning sensation of being suspended in midair before landing and plunging down the slope.

It was a fun, thrilling experience for those of us looking at the screen, leaning left or right, and tilting forward or back with the movements of the movie and the theater. However, about five minutes into the experience, I heard a bit of commotion coming from the back row. There were muffled sounds of knocking and sliding, and gasps that were more distressed than thrilled. As the simulated skiing grew more intense in front of us, so did the sounds of protest coming from behind. There was more knocking about, alarmed exclamations of "Oooh!" and a very familiar "Crap!!" My brother kept his eyes intently forward, but at one point I had to turn and look. At the back of the little theater, illuminated by the light of the screen, was our mom, turned sideways and halfway out of her seat. She wasn't looking at the screen. With one hand pressed against the back wall and the other pushing on the low ceiling, she was bracing herself, attempting to keep from moving, as the little theater shook, bounced, and tilted wildly from side to side. Her feet kept slipping out from under her into the tiny aisle, but instead of just falling back into her seat, for some reason she kept trying to stay upright. I turned back toward the screen and, like my brother, spent the remainder of the fifteen minutes trying to convey that I had no relationship to the woman in the last row. When the lights came on at the end of our experience, her purse had made its way all the way down the aisle and come to rest near my feet. Later, my mom would get much better at letting go, and even leaning in, but this experience will forever come to mind when I think about the struggle to control the uncontrollable.

CHAPTER 8

Tilting Toward Acceptance

If resistance and struggle are ways of saying no to your feelings, letting go and leaning in are the beginnings of saying yes to them. This openness to feeling your feelings without judgment, and without trying to change them, creates space for the next step, which involves more fully accepting your thoughts. Saying yes to your thoughts can be a little different from saying yes to your feelings. Feelings are fairly straightforward. The thing to do with feelings is to feel them. Thoughts, on the other hand, can appear to be one thing when they are really something else. Because of cognitive fusion, the alarm appears to be the fire; the map is confused with the territory. This leads to the struggle to control and avoid thoughts that we've identified as "Pure O" OCD. The opposite of that struggle, which starts with letting go and leaning in, continues with the acceptance of the thought.

Acceptance Through Cognitive Defusion

"Acceptance" of a thought does not mean buying or believing the thought. It does, however, mean being willing to have or experience the thought. How do we make room for thoughts that we find painful or frightening? As we'll learn throughout this chapter, it's all about using the process of cognitive defusion.

Many years ago, I was in a pretty serious car wreck. I was driving alone through an empty intersection when a much larger car coming from my left ran the light, slamming into my driver's side door. My car was knocked diagonally across the intersection, where it hit a lamppost head on. My windshield was shattered and my car totaled, but aside from some cuts and bruises, I was fine. The occupants of the other car were completely uninjured. Afterward, for the first few days, I found it uncomfortable to think about the accident. I remember having trouble sleeping for a couple of nights, as memories of the crash made me jumpy and anxious. Talking about it was also upsetting. I didn't like having to describe exactly what happened. As I told the story to more people, however, something started to change. I began to include more details, setting the stage a bit by explaining that it was late at night, and I had just gotten off work. My language became more descriptive and less accurate. When I described what happened to my car immediately after it was hit, I said that it "flew" across the intersection and "wrapped around" a lamppost, neither of which were literally true. I also started to play up amusing details, like the fact that I was careful to turn off my headlights before exiting my car. With repetition, not only did the story become easier to tell, it became somewhat enjoyable to tell. As I have continued to tell the story over the years, it has slowly been transformed in my experience from an event into a narrative. The story of my "bad wreck," as well as my memory of it, has slowly separated itself from the actual event, taking on a separate life of its own. Today, the event, like the rest of my life history, exists exclusively in story form. My anxious brain recognizes the memories and thoughts about the accident as a familiar story. This story has little to do with my current life, even when I'm driving through a lonely intersection late at night.

This is defusion as it occurs naturally. Allowing ourselves to think about, and even talk about, a trauma helps us to process the actual event into the memory or narrative that it will be going forward. This transformation of reality into language, and the repetition or stylizing of that language into a narrative, is how breaking news slowly becomes history. It's through this process that the events of our lives become the stories of our lives, composed and organized into a form that we can live comfortably with. We compile these stories into chapters or volumes, then place them on a shelf for future reference. The tools presented in this chapter all tap into this natural process of transformation.

In ACT, these tools are often referred to as "defusion methods." They can include anything that helps you experience your thoughts as thoughts, rather than as the reality they refer to. Versions of these methods, like the use of humor, or sharing our thoughts with a friend, are skills that most people develop and use intuitively to make room for difficult thoughts. The techniques presented here have been developed as part of ACT over the past thirty years. Using them successfully requires a certain amount of experimentation. A method that works well for one person may not be as helpful for another. I often find that the specific methods patients come to on their own are the ones that work best for them. With this in mind, rather than just giving instructions for the "top ten defusion methods," I'd like to convey a more general sense of what these methods look like. I'll offer a few examples, focusing on how you can effectively apply them to specific thoughts. Then, I'll encourage you to develop defusion methods of your own.

Observing and Reporting

The most basic defusion methods involve capturing our thoughts as words and gaining some distance from them. This usually involves condensing or summarizing what we're thinking into a short phrase, or even a single word.

I'm Having the Thought…

A very straightforward way to highlight that what we are experiencing is just a thought is by prefacing the thought with words that emphasize its thought-like nature. For example, when Anthony finally decided to start wearing his jacket again, he began by observing, out loud, "*I'm having the thought that* this jacket is contaminated by old-guy snot." Sophie was able to gain some distance from her obsessions by saying something like "My *mind* is questioning my love for my parents." This is straightforward reporting of our experience, but with the clarification that what we are describing is a thought, not a reality. Instead of saying, "Eventually Adam and I will grow apart," Lou learned to more accurately report his thoughts by saying something like "*I'm imagining* an older version of my son who is less close to me." This is a very simple way to create a bit of space between you and your experience, and a good method to start with.

Try it now. Pick a disturbing, obsessive, or worrisome thought. First, state it as a fact: "I'm going to fail." Then try stating it with the thinking qualifier: "I'm having the thought that I am going to fail." Notice how the more qualified reporting of your thoughts makes them easier to accept as thoughts.

Looking at Thoughts

Another way to get this distance from your thoughts is to write them down. We're not talking about journaling here. That's a different process, which can be helpful in many cases, but can also be like obsessing or ruminating on paper. Instead, try to capture the gist of your obsessive thoughts in a single sentence, or better yet, a phrase. Write that down and look at it. Try writing it again, larger or smaller. Write it in a different color ink, or using your nondominant hand. All of these are ways to help you begin to look *at* these thoughts instead of *through* them. Pick up the paper that the words are written on. Notice that no matter what you write on the paper, no matter how painful or harsh the words, the paper still has the same weight in your hands. Words, thoughts, judgments, and stories are all as weightless as they are transitory. The power we associate with them lies elsewhere. Fold the paper and put it in your pocket. Carry it around all day, looking at it whenever you happen to remember it. How hard is it to just carry your obsessive thoughts with you? Do they get heavier or lighter as the day goes by? Try writing them repeatedly on a few post-it notes, and then stick the notes on the walls of your home. Leave them there for a few hours, or even a few days. What happens to the power of these words over time? Is it possible for them to exist as just another part of your environment, like wallpaper?

Hearing Thoughts

Another group of defusion methods involves speaking or singing your obsessive thoughts out loud until the words begin to separate from the reality they are stuck to. Use the same obsessive or troubling thought, distilled into a phrase or a word. Now pick a simple tune, like "Happy Birthday to You" or "Row, Row, Row Your Boat," and sing the thoughts over and over again to that tune. This is one of those things that you just have to try. Some things are understood better through experience than through explanation. Try this now, and notice what happens to your experience of the troubling thoughts as you sing them. What becomes of the power attached to the words?

A variety of defusion methods involve saying upsetting or obsessive thoughts out loud in different ways until this defusion occurs, to a greater or lesser degree. For example, when Anthony decided to work on wearing that "contaminated" jacket, we spent a little time with the word "snot." I'll ask you to do the same thing I asked Anthony to do. Close your eyes and say the word "snot" slowly a couple of times. Notice what your experience is as you do this. Is there a general feeling of grossness that accompanies this word? Does a particular image come to mind? Maybe a specific color? What about a consistency? Is it slippery? Sticky? Do you notice a slight congested feeling in your nose or chest? Can you sort of feel something snotty on your skin? For Anthony, and for me, the answer to these questions was yes. Certain words have a particular kind of power. They evoke. They *in*voke. They manifest. Like magic.

Now try this. Focus on the imagery and feelings, the whole snotty experience that the word "snot" evokes, and then repeat the word "snot" out loud about once a second for thirty seconds. I know it feels silly, but just do it, and pay attention to what happens... Listen to the sound of the word as it comes from your mouth. Feel the air moving between your tongue and the roof of your mouth with the "s" sound, and the "n" vibrating slightly in your sinuses. Notice what happens to the snot-related images and feelings as you continue to repeat the word rhythmically. What becomes of all that snottyness? For Anthony, and for me, with repetition, the word, and the thought, lost much of its thick, green, slimy, ickyness. "Snot" becomes more like a noise. A noise made by your mouth, but also by your mind. Now try saying it a few times very slowly, in a deep voice, like a record played back at a slower speed. Try speeding it up, rapid and high-pitched. Now pick your own sticky thought, maybe something related to an obsession. It might be more than a single word, possibly a whole phrase. Try playing with your thought in the same way. What happens to your experience of the thought?

For Sophie, the condensed version of her most frightening and disturbing obsession was "I'm a sociopath." The first time I asked her to say it out loud in one of our sessions, she couldn't do it without crying. The words were so powerful in her experience of them that she burst into tears when she spoke them. With just a little practice, however, she was able to say the words with a lightness and playfulness that made both of us giggle. She developed a sort of lilting prattle around the word "sociopath" that went something like this: "Sociopath, sociopathic, socio, socio, path, path, pathic. Sociopathapic, pathiososhic. So chic! Sociopathic... She sells socio sea shells at the sociopathic seashore." Later, Sophie noticed that the word sociopath made her think of socialites walking along a path. When she said the word, she imagined young girls at a cotillion proceeding down a flower-lined path in white dresses. When she noticed herself obsessing about whether she might be a sociopath, she came to refer to it as "heading down the socio path again," and imagined herself walking along in a white dress, smiling demurely. The image made her smile. In those moments, the painful narrative that the thought formerly represented seemed obscure and remote to Sophie. The defusion of the thought from all that it was formerly attached to made it easier for Sophie to accept the thought, not as a reality, but as a thought. Freed from the need to struggle with the thought, Sophie was able to notice other things, including feelings of love for her parents, which she felt in different ways at different times.

Don't Touch That Dial!

Other defusion methods create space around a thought by emphasizing the separation of self from experience. These methods emphasize the relational, two-entity quality of consciousness. There's us and then there's our thoughts. This makes room for us to notice exactly what relationship exists between ourselves and a particular thought. One way to do this is to assign a name to the thinking part of your mind, clearly distinguishing it from *you*. In teaching about this defusion method, Steve Hayes famously refers to his mind as "George." When it offers warnings, judgments, or other thoughts that aren't helpful, Steve responds with a gracious "Thanks, George, but I've got this…" Thanking your mind for a thought, even an unpleasant, anxious one, is a great way to tilt away from struggle and toward acceptance. There are any number of ways to highlight that obsessive thoughts are not *you.*

Doom Radio

Whatever your political leanings, these days it's easy to find a media outlet that expresses the exact opposite of your views. Reading or listening to a bias that runs counter to your own can easily evoke annoyance or even outrage. Now, imagine that you lived or worked in a setting where the television or radio was tuned to that particular station much of the day, and you were unable to control the volume or turn it off. Would you watch or listen attentively all day long, just steeping in your indignation at what you were hearing? This would probably get old. Instead, you would probably find other things to do and go about your business. Would you feel the need to contact the commentator and try to change their views? Or would you allow them to say whatever they wanted to say, secure in the knowledge that their views were not your own? This is not unlike what happens when we notice that certain thoughts are a product of our threat-biased, anxious mind. I like to think of this part of the mind as *DOOM Radio.* "That's D-O-O-M, folks. All bad news, all the time. Keeping you posted on all the ways you and your life are totally screwed." We all have this station on our dial. Some of us are just more tuned into it, or happen to get a clearer signal. That doesn't mean we have to listen attentively and hang on every word. Try this: Notice the thoughts from the anxious part of your mind, but imagine them coming through in the voice of the most annoying TV or radio personality you can imagine. Let yourself hear the words dripping with sarcasm and smart-assness. For Lou, this radio station featured only one program, which focused exclusively on the future of his relationship with his son. Lou imagined the host of the program to be a boorish slob of a fellow who knew just how to get under Lou's skin. As a defusion exercise, Lou intentionally imagined his obsessive thoughts adapted to the program's format:

Host: Today we're going to be talking to a future version of Lou's only son, Adam. Twenty-year-old Adam is joining us by phone from the college he chose to attend on the coast *opposite* the coast his old man lives on (*scornful sniggering*). Now Adam, can you tell us exactly when it was that you first started to feel like you couldn't stand to be around your dad?

Adam: Who? (*laughing*)

Host: (*Loud chortling*) Now, come on Adam, you remember that annoying balding guy who lives with your mom…

Lou worked with this exercise extensively, noting that the program's theme song was the sentimental folk ballad "Cat's in the Cradle." The show's only sponsor was Hallmark, and all the commercials had to do with the "empty nest" of Lou's future. Imagining these thoughts as coming from a very biased, one-note source helped Lou to experience them as a worst-case expression of his fears and not representative of his real relationship with Adam. Since the host of the program was not him, Lou didn't have to respond to the thoughts by arguing, convincing, or reassuring. He could also notice the contrast between this radio program, as it played in the background, and his experience of reading a bedtime story to his son, or playing with Adam on the beach. Over time, it became clearer to Lou that one had little to do with the other. Lou was able to identify his avoidance of Adam or his compulsive reassurance seeking as efforts to "change the channel" and escape from his obsessive thoughts. Experiencing these thoughts as "not me" made it easier for Lou to accept them, making the avoidance less necessary.

Muzak

Another way to defuse from obsessive thoughts, particularly when they have a repetitive quality, is to imagine them as background noise or music. The term I like to use for this is "Muzak," a registered trademark for an American brand of background music dating back to the 1930s. I think it's a wonderful word for something that is not exactly noise, but not exactly music, either. Think about the music you hear in the background when you're shopping at the supermarket or almost any store. How invested or interested are you in what exactly is playing? Do you really go to Target for the music? If we let them, obsessive thoughts can be a lot like Muzak. They are what we experience, in the background, when we are doing something else.

I like the word so much that I apply it to anything that exists in the background of awareness. Heartbeats, traffic noise, swallowing saliva, the feeling of clothes on your skin...all Muzak. Defusion means adding repetitive, obsessive thoughts to this category. We choose to treat certain parts of our experience as meaningless background noise all the time. For example, have you ever noticed the sounds that your refrigerator makes? You may have noticed that they're fairly constant, but have you ever just sat and listened to those sounds for a while, very closely? Have you tried to figure out exactly what makes those sounds? Have you replayed them to yourself when you were away from the refrigerator, or tried to imitate them for a close friend? Have you ever tried writing them down? No? Wait...are you saying that you just hear these sounds without getting involved with them in any particular way? Are you saying that you neither love nor hate these sounds, and don't make any particular effort to stop them? This is hearing without listening, and we do it all the time. Refrigerator sounds are a form of Muzak. Now try imagining what it would be like if your refrigerator happened to make sounds that sounded exactly like your obsessive thoughts. For Anthony, it might be a continuous "snotty-snot-snot," or for Sophie a more clunky "soci-path-ic, love-less ingrate..." Carl's refrigerator was making the nonsensical yet somber sound of "drink-spiking rapist." You get the idea. You might not particularly like what you're hearing, but since it's just Muzak, whether made by your refrigerator or your mind, how big of a problem does it have to be?

The TV Across the Room

When our obsessive thoughts are images, it can help to imagine watching them on a television screen. Sit for a few minutes and watch them playing on the small screen, perhaps in a loop. I like to imagine an older TV set, with a bit of static or scrolling, which reminds me that these are just images. Then imagine moving away from the TV. You can still see it, but it's at the other end of a long room. Now notice what else is in the room. Are there people there? What are they doing? Can you still see the TV? Can you let these images play, without struggling to change the channel, and go on with the business of living your life? Does it really matter what's on that little screen on the other side of the room? In fact, does it even matter if it's a bigger screen?

As the context for your thoughts, *you* are the room itself. The images on the TV are merely part of the ever-changing content of the room. As you notice more of your experience, more things in the room, the room actually gets bigger. The TV is still part of your experience, but it's a smaller part of it, relative to the size of the room. The amazing thing about consciousness is that it can expand indefinitely. No matter how big your thoughts or your anxiety, *you* always have the option of being bigger than they are. It's only the struggle to limit or control what you are aware of that makes things feel crowded. When you have your nose pressed up against the TV screen and are trying desperately to change the channel, the images on the screen seem huge and threatening. When you let go of this struggle and make room for more of your experience, the thoughts become a smaller part of your world.

Going Over the Top

You may have noticed that some of these defusion methods have a humorous quality. This is not a coincidence. Humor is, in many ways, a natural method of defusion. Most of us recognize humor as a mechanism that relieves stress and tension. When we laugh, the diaphragm contracts in an audible way as part of a parasympathetic response, helping the body to recover from fight-or-flight arousal. The *incongruity-resolution theory* of humor asserts that humor occurs when our brain perceives an incongruity between a concept and the reality that the concept refers to (Attardo 2017). Does this sound familiar? Most humor is based on things that make us slightly uncomfortable: sex, violence, conflict, or even just inconvenience. Think about the setup portion of your standard joke, or the opening "Have you ever noticed how..." portion of a stand-up comic's monologue. A situation is presented that involves some tension or uncertainty. The humor happens when elements of this uncomfortable situation are exaggerated beyond what is realistic (the punch line). Our anxious brain, which has been put slightly on alert by the setup, realizes suddenly that this is "just a joke." In other words, only a narrative, not real. The relief we feel is what makes us smile or laugh. The implication of this theory is that cognitive defusion not only gives us relief from anxiety but can be funny as well. Humor is a form of defusion.

Using humor to defuse from obsessive thoughts involves looking directly at those thoughts and moving *toward* them. It's a form of leaning in, and it can be a little scary at first. That's because this is the setup part of the joke. If you're open to it, think of a troublesome thought that frequently plagues you. Then, sort of going along with the thought, see if you can take it to the next level, exaggerating the most uncomfortable parts of the thought. If this only makes you more uncomfortable, exaggerate a bit more, taking the thought "over the top."

I incorporate this type of defusion a lot when working with patients who have phobias. When a patient with a fear of heights reports thoughts of falling, I'll ask them to imagine falling in very slow motion, or imagine themselves bouncing when they hit the ground, like a rubber ball. For the person with a dog phobia, I'll ask them to describe in detail what it would look like if they were mauled by the chihuahua that they just crossed the street to avoid. Obsessive thoughts can be even easier to use humor with, because most people with obsessions already experience them as somewhat exaggerated or extreme. Taking them just a bit further can tip them into the territory of ridiculous. If all this sounds like I'm suggesting that you "make fun" of your obsessive thoughts, it's because that's pretty much what I'm saying.

Part of what makes this effective is that the process requires us to interact in an intentional way with thoughts that we might otherwise struggle to push away. This amounts to letting go of our struggle with the thoughts, and leaning into them. When we do this, it becomes clear that what we're dealing with are simply words and images. I once worked with a patient who struggled with intrusive thoughts that took the form of disturbing violent and sexual images. While they changed from week to week, at any given time, he was usually on guard against at least one recurring image. During our early sessions, he would sometimes jump slightly in his seat and grimace when these images came into his mind. He had a variety of subtle internal rituals that were efforts to "block" these upsetting thoughts. At first, he was hesitant to tell me what the images were, but this changed over time. Eventually, after a particularly vigorous episode of shuddering and grimacing, he whispered confidingly that the image he was struggling with that week was of "a penis being sliced." Being careful not to shudder myself, I leaned in toward him, lowered my own voice, and asked what, to me, was the obvious question. "Now, when you say *sliced*...do you mean *lengthwise?* Or are we talking about cross-sections, like how you slice a banana into a bowl of cereal?" While I waited for him to answer, this gentleman gave me the oddest look, then burst out laughing. I joined him, and we ended up in tears. It turns out, it had not occurred to him that there is more than one way to slice a penis. Choosing to be playful with thoughts demonstrates to the anxious brain that these thoughts are not actually dangerous. Humor allows us to view even the most "unacceptable" thoughts from a slightly different angle, making room for them as just thoughts.

Exposure as Defusion

Perhaps the most concrete way to tilt toward acceptance is by taking action that brings us into direct contact with experiences that we would otherwise avoid. Exposure to feared objects, situations, and thoughts is the heart of traditional behavior therapy for OCD. In that context, the purpose of exposure is to allow for habituation to these experiences. By placing yourself in the situation, touching the feared object, or sitting with the uncomfortable thought, you allow the fight-or-flight response to "extinguish" itself. Exposure has a role in ACT, but the focus is a little different. Instead of just waiting for the anxiety program to rewrite itself through repeated exposure, which is ultimately a change on the content level, ACT focuses on helping you make a shift at the context level. Instead of focusing on whether or not your anxiety is going down during exposure, which is standard practice in traditional exposure methods, the focus is on being more open to your experience and letting go of the struggle to control it. Exposure is an opportunity to observe your anxious thoughts and feelings in a defused way.

From an ACT perspective, contact with feared situations and objects can allow our thoughts and judgments to separate themselves from these situations and objects. In other words, exposure itself can act as a defusion method. It's almost a truism that any dreaded event, whether undergoing a root canal, doing your taxes, or attending a professional mixer, is never quite as bad as you imagine it will be. The *idea* of the event is almost always worse than the actual experience. We covered the reasons for this in chapter one. Your anxious brain wants to prepare you for the worst possible outcome, so it offers you thoughts that are biased in that direction. In effect, your thoughts are attempting to warn you away from these experiences, no matter how valuable they may be to you. When you move forward and actually have the experience, it's hard to reconcile it with the more dire thoughts that you had about it. As a consequence, the thoughts become unstuck from the actual events.

Because of this focus on defusion, the ACT version of exposure tends to be a little more lighthearted and playful than the traditional behavioral therapy version. We've spent quite a bit of time on Anthony's jacket and his thoughts about old-guy snot. However, snot was just one of Anthony's contamination concerns. A much more serious issue was fecal matter. Shit, crap, poo…whatever you care to call it, Anthony wanted nothing to do with it. He even had trouble dealing with his own feces. He was particularly obsessed with poo that he saw on the sidewalk as he walked around the city. Here, he encountered a hierarchy of troubling turds. On the lower end was poo that was small, dry, and obviously produced by a dog. On the higher end, anxiety-wise, was larger, wetter poo that might possibly have come from a human being. The compulsive component of Anthony's OCD included carefully scanning the sidewalk for signs of poo, and giving it a wide berth. He would routinely backtrack and cross the street if he even thought he saw turds ahead. He also avoided using public restrooms, and when he did use them, sought out urinals rather than proper sit-down toilets.

As exposure, Anthony and I developed a game in which we ranked sidewalk turds from 1 to 10 points, depending on how fresh and human-sourced they appeared to be. The more disturbing the turd, the higher the score. Between sessions, when either of us came across a high-ranking turd on the sidewalk, we took a picture of it with our phones and sent the pictures to each other, along with our proposed "turd score." I tended to defer to Anthony for the accuracy of these rankings. This exposure game required Anthony first to get close enough to the sidewalk poo to get a clear picture of it, then to have the added exposure of carrying the image on his phone, and finally to look at it to assign a score and share it with me. Interacting with the poo in this way, along with the game-like quality of the exercise, shifted the context of Anthony's interaction with the poo that he saw. Over time, he began to actively seek out the very sort of turds he had previously avoided. To further defuse from his obsessive thoughts about poo of questionable provenance, Anthony practiced intentionally developing "backstories" for certain turds, imagining what sort of person might have laid them, including the person's sex, age, weight, profession, and dietary preferences. Later in treatment, Anthony completed a survey of public toilets around the city, giving them one to five "stars" based on the condition in which he found them, and taking photos of the most befouled, five-star toilets he came across.

The Silliness Factor

As powerful and helpful as these tools are, one obstacle to using them that I have encountered repeatedly over the years is that many of them can seem a little awkward or silly. No matter how clear patients may be about the theory behind their use, some are hesitant to practice or even to try defusion methods for this reason. It's not just the silliness factor, though. On the surface, these methods can appear rather gimmicky or too simple to be effective. To overcome this hesitancy, I've learned to start by emphasizing that, at its best, defusion is something that happens naturally all the time. We use a range of "natural" defusion methods intuitively to help us accept uncomfortable thoughts and ideas. Most of these methods involve some form of storytelling, often with intentional distortions, as happened with the story of my car wreck. When we share our thoughts with others, emphasizing their exaggerated or unrealistic elements, we experience those thoughts more as thoughts and less as reality. As we have seen, humor is often based on this playful exaggeration of thoughts that make us uncomfortable. Our playful interaction with the thoughts helps the anxious brain to recognize them as thoughts, rather than the dangerous or uncomfortable reality that they refer to. Because the defusion methods presented here are techniques, they are stylized versions of these more natural practices, designed to focus and facilitate the natural process of defusion. A certain amount of gimmickry is a necessary byproduct of that stylization. As for the silliness, if using these methods makes you laugh, that's just an added bonus.

Tilting…

We tend to think of acceptance as a state of peace and equanimity that comes to us over time. "At first I was struggling with the idea, but over time I came to accept it." In this view, acceptance is a gradual process that we wait for. When it comes to changes in circumstances or events that involve loss, this view of acceptance makes sense. Nature has provided us with the ability to habituate to alarming or painful changes, and this is indeed a process that happens over time. However, this is a rather passive way to think about acceptance, and not as helpful when we're talking about accepting your thoughts and feelings right now, in the moment. "Acceptance," as it is used here, the A of our LLAMP, is not so much a state or goal as a "move" that you can make right now—a shift or tilt that involves looking at and making room for your obsessive thoughts. This becomes more possible when we experience thoughts as what they are, rather than as what they say they are. Defusion creates space in which to make the move of saying yes to your experience.

Going back to our image of the person in the middle of a see-saw, this "yes" tilts your energy away from resistance and struggle and sends it in another direction. Accepting your thoughts and feelings allows you to make choices that move you toward creating and living a life that you value. You can think of acceptance as the fulcrum on which this see-saw pivots. I've borrowed this idea of "pivoting" directly from Steve Hayes. He uses it very effectively as the central metaphor for change in his rich and accessible book *A Liberated Mind: How to Pivot Toward What Matters* (Hayes 2019). In it, he points out that "pivot" originally referred to the pin in a hinge.

> Pivots in hinges take the energy that is headed in one direction and immediately redirect it in another. When we pivot, we take the energy inside an inflexible process and channel it toward a flexible one. (23)

I've turned Steve's hinge on its side and extended the parts into a see-saw, but the pivoting and the transfer of energy from one direction to another still rests on the fulcrum of acceptance.

All of the LLAMP skills facilitate this shift of energy. Labeling and Letting go tilt us away from struggling. Acceptance of our thoughts swings that energy toward a Mindfulness of the present and connection with our values and Purpose. With practice, the movement through these steps becomes increasingly fluid. Hayes (2019) compares the components of ACT to dance steps that combine to form a seamless whole:

> As you practice the skills, you develop increasing flexibility. And just as it is easier to swing your partner around if your partner is always in fluid motion, rather than stopping after each move, by continuously developing your flexibility skills, you become increasingly able to take the energy of your existing thoughts and feelings, even the negative ones, and swing them into energy for growth. (24)

This analogy of ACT as dancing resonates with my experience both personally and as an ACT therapist. After thirty years of using and teaching these steps to patients, I have to agree that the whole process feels very much like learning to dance. After a while, there is a sense of rhythm and flow.

Making Your Own Acceptance Move

As you experiment with the defusion methods described here, allow yourself to be creative and adapt them to your own circumstances. Defusion methods lend themselves to creativity and novelty. Keep in mind that this is all about getting to the point of saying yes to your thoughts. Not *Yes, I agree with you,* but more like *Yes, you said that,* and *Yes, you've said that before,* and *Yes, thank you for sharing.* Remember, it's just a tilt. If "yes" is too far, try just a nod and an *Okaaaay...* Don't worry about being silly. Silly actually helps a lot here. Start by just reporting your experience: *I'm having the thought that* _____. Then try writing the thoughts down. Carry them in your pocket or stick them to the wall. You can even put them in your shoe and walk around on them. Try saying the thoughts out loud, over and over again, for a minute or two. Try doing them in different voices. Sing them, loudly. If you have trouble finding privacy, do it in the shower or in your car, but do it. You can't really know if something is likely to help until you've actually tried it, maybe even several times.

Put your obsessive, anxious thoughts into the mouth of another, imaginary person. Or a lizard. Since many anxious thoughts come from our more primal "lizard brain," try imagining a little lizard saying these things to you. I keep a tiny plastic lizard in my office to help patients imagine this. See if you can hear your obsessions as Muzak, piped in through some invisible speakers, just faintly, but constantly, in the background. Imagine hearing your obsessions humming out from the back of your fridge. Lean into these thoughts with humor and playfulness. It might feel like false bravado at first, but eventually the bravery will be more real. Look for opportunities to take real-life behavioral steps toward things you avoid because of your obsessions. Notice the thoughts that fly up like little flares warning you away from this exposure. Thank your mind for the warning, and lean in further. Play with the thoughts that arise to show your mind that thoughts really aren't that dangerous. Make room for this energy coming from the struggling, avoidant part of your mind and tilt it in a whole new direction.

CHAPTER 9

Bringing in the World

I hope the stories you've read so far offer a sense of the various forms that "Pure O" obsessions can take, and the subtle rituals and avoidance that can accompany them. What's harder to describe is the ongoing day-to-day experience of obsessive thinking. For Anthony, simply wearing a particular article of clothing involved navigating an array of disgusting images and hearing contamination narratives playing on a continual loop. When immersed in this private drama, he had trouble hearing the music he was listening to or seeing the colorful urban landscape he was running through. Sophie could spend hours contemplating the implications of being a sociopath, her inner monologues leaving her spacey and distracted even as she tried to spend quality time with her parents. Lou moved through his days privately struggling to connect with the aloof "future Adam" in his head, even as the "present Adam" in his life struggled to hold his attention. Similarly, Judy had trouble really engaging with her dorm mates because she was so engrossed with her private horror movie of academic failure. Miguel struggled to focus at work and then was distracted at home as he lived through an endless variety of hypothetical futures. At times, jobs he had not even applied for and women he had never met seemed more real to him than his actual job and the woman he lived with. Finally, Carl was so vigilant to fending off any thoughts of women that might be harmful or disrespectful that he failed to notice how caring and respectful his interactions with actual women tended to be. These are just a few examples of the recurring, ongoing, extended engagement with an imaginary, internal world that is obsessive thinking. Living in your head comes at the cost of experiencing fully the rich sensations, lived experiences, and intimate connections of life in the actual world. This chapter is all about increasing your awareness of and connection to what is real, even as you tilt away from that engrossing engagement with life "in your head."

Mindfulness

As important as it is, I tend to wait until later in treatment to discuss mindfulness with my patients. Of the five skills covered in this book, mindfulness is the one that people tend to have the least patience for. This is why it comes second to last in our LLAMP acronym (that, and the fact that LMLAP is harder to pronounce). Anxious people in particular sometimes want to skip over mindfulness. The response I get most often is some version of "Oh yes, I've heard this before. I agree, being in the moment is very important. Now what's the next step?" For many people, the idea of practicing and developing mindfulness sounds time-consuming and tedious. If you happen to be one of those people, perhaps you should start by just (you guessed it) sitting with that thought for a moment. Notice everything that comes to your awareness when the topic of mindfulness is introduced. Do you notice a tensing up anywhere in your body? Are there judgments that just happen to arise? Next, consider this: is it possible that this discomfort and desire to skip over mindfulness and get on to thinking and doing other things could be the very reason to spend a little more time on this particular chapter?

When thoughts become obsessions, our relationship to them is characterized by struggle. We struggle with these thoughts because we perceive them as a threat, but it's also true that we perceive them as a threat because we are struggling with them. In the midst of the struggle, obsessive thoughts can carry more weight and seem more real than other aspects of our experience. When you are "in your head" in this way, you are more aware of the narratives and images that make up the obsessive thoughts than of the wind on your face, the ground beneath your feet, or the food in your mouth. In these moments, there is not enough space between you and the obsessive thoughts for other parts of your experience to fully register in your awareness. Stepping back from your thoughts enough to notice all of your experience in a given moment is the essence of mindfulness. It is the opposite of being "in your head." If you imagine an obsessive thought as a particular area or spot in the field of your experience, you can think of your awareness as a circle that surrounds and includes that spot. The struggle to control or eliminate a thought tightens the circle of your awareness around that spot, making it a bigger, more central part of your experience. Mindfulness is the opposite of limiting your experience in this way. It's about expanding the circle of your awareness to include more. When this happens, the obsessive thought becomes a smaller part, proportionally, of your experience overall.

The word "mindfulness" has enjoyed a surge of popularity over the past two decades. Like any word subjected to heavy use, it has taken on a broad spectrum of meaning. For some, it refers to a specific practice or discipline that often centers around meditation. For others, it's more of a general state of awareness cultivated in daily life. Most would agree that it involves being more fully "in the moment" and meeting your experience of *now* without attachment or judgment. From an ACT perspective, this means observing your experience with the awareness that none of this is *you*, and experiencing thoughts as thoughts, separate from what they refer to. Mindfulness helps us to shift from struggling with obsessive thoughts and anxiety to experiencing them with more openness and acceptance. In this way, mindfulness happens from the perspective of the self-as-context and is very much about our relationship to the content of our experience.

The Refuge of Now

For most people, most of the time, the present moment is not a bad place to be. If you're not extremely warm or terribly cold, if you're not very hungry or thirsty, and if you're not in a great deal of pain, *right now* can be a refuge, even as difficulties and challenges continue to be a part of your life. When it comes to thoughts and feelings, suffering is usually focused on events that happened before the present moment or things that we expect will happen sometime in the future. In the present, we are not really experiencing these past or future events. When we are fully in the present moment, both the past and the future exist only as thoughts.

Most obsessive thoughts involve narratives or images that refer to the past or the future. This is true of Anthony's images of snot or poo, Sophie's lack of tears at her parents' joint funeral, and the story of Lou's weakening bond with Adam. Mindfulness means accepting the mind's stories about the past and narratives about the future the same way we accept our breathing, the beating of our hearts, and the warmth of the sun on our skin as an experience of the moment.

While the term "mindfulness" may be unfamiliar or even exotic to some, most of us have experience with finding refuge in the present moment. For many people, this comes with certain activities that require a degree of focus and paying attention. For me, cooking is a good example. Perhaps because I'm not a particularly skilled cook, successful cooking requires a lot of focus and attention to what I'm doing. Not only do I have to measure and count, I have to attend to things like color, smell, and consistency. When I'm cooking, I'm facilitating a process in which ingredients are transformed into something more. When I'm fully engaged with that process, not only is the outcome more likely to be edible, but I'm less likely to be caught up in ruminations about things that happened earlier or worries about things that will happen later.

This absorption or engagement with an ongoing process is what many people refer to as being "in the zone" of an activity. The refuge it provides is an important part of what many people value about participating in certain sports that require their full attention, or playing a musical instrument. It's part of the appeal of many crafting activities, like knitting or woodwork. It's also what many people find soothing about listening to music, hiking, or interacting with a beloved dog or cat. All of these activities offer a richness of experience in the present moment that is separate from stories or narratives about the past or the future. They invite us to pay more attention to what is happening now, which helps us to experience the stories and narratives as not happening now.

Mindfulness and LLAMP

As the "M" in LLAMP, mindfulness involves skills that can increase your awareness of and grounding in the current moment. A certain degree of mindfulness is implicit, however, in the first three skills as well. As soon as you remember the LLAMP acronym and start to use the skills by labeling your experience in some way, you are practicing mindfulness. Labeling brings with it an increased focus on and attention to the thing that we are labeling, settling us more fully into the moment. In fact, a common meditation from the Buddhist tradition consists of sitting quietly, observing your experience, and labeling it. For example, if you notice your breath, simply say "breathing" silently to yourself. If you become aware of an itch on your face, say "itching." When you notice an anxious thought, you might label this "anxiety." Letting go and leaning in also involve a degree of mindfulness. The openness to experience that comes with letting go of struggle and control is part of adopting a mindful stance. Leaning into our experience involves attending and focusing in a mindful way. And, finally, the acceptance move described in the previous chapter, along with the defusion methods that facilitate it, tilts us toward experiencing our thoughts without judgment, which is also an important part of mindfulness.

So, as you have been practicing the Label, Let go, and Accept skills, you have already begun to practice mindfulness. The skills presented in this chapter will help you to settle more fully into the current moment, connecting and staying with the fullness of your experience of that moment. When you are moved to use the LLAMP skills, you are already quite aware of your thoughts and feelings, though often in a reactive, struggling way. The Label, Let go, and Accept skills are oriented toward shifting your relationship to those thoughts and feelings from one of struggle to one of willingness. The Mindfulness step is about making room for those thoughts and feelings as well as everything else that is part of the current moment.

It looks something like this: Using LLAMP as a guide, you notice and label "anxious feelings" and "obsessive thoughts." You take a breath and let go of the struggle to control those feelings and thoughts, instead leaning into your experience of them. You might say to yourself, I am having the thought that…or use some other defusion method to unstick the thought from what it refers to, tilting you toward accepting the thought. Now, using mindfulness, notice what else you are aware of. What sensations are you aware of in your body? Where are you? What do you see? What do you hear? Bringing more of the world into your awareness makes the anxious feelings and obsessive thoughts part of a larger whole. In the current moment, narratives that refer to past or future exist only as thoughts. In this way, mindfulness supports further defusion of these thoughts from the reality they refer to.

Wading into Mindfulness

In my work with anxious patients, incorporating mindfulness into treatment can be tricky in two different ways. For patients with little or no familiarity with mindfulness as a concept, the idea of learning to meditate can be a little intimidating, or even off-putting. They may be concerned that they won't be able to find the time or the privacy to practice, or may just consider the whole notion a bit too "woo-woo" for them. Then there are the patients who have considerable experience with meditation or who practice it regularly. They often have a tendency to think of mindfulness as something you do during meditation, and that developing mindfulness means meditating more and better. For both the uninitiated and the veteran, equating mindfulness with the practice of meditation can be somewhat problematic.

While meditation is an excellent way to develop mindfulness skills, it is far from the only way. What's more, if mindfulness is something you only practice during meditation, it's likely to be of limited help when dealing with anxiety that comes up at other times. Running off to meditate as a response to anxiety can quickly start to look like avoidance, or even a compulsive ritual. I think of meditation as a little like going to a gym and working out. For most of us, the value in working out is not to become really good at lifting weights and running on treadmills. Instead, these are efficient ways to become strong and fit so that we can do the things in life that we value outside of the gym. Meditation is a way to work out and develop our mindfulness "muscles" so that we can use them effectively as we live our lives outside of our meditation practice. Just as there are other ways to stay strong and fit than going to the gym, there are many ways to become more mindful other than meditation. To avoid this trap of "mindfulness = meditation," I tend to begin any conversation about mindfulness by simply having patients focus more on their sensory experiences, starting with simple experiences and slowly increasing their complexity. When it comes to being mindful of their own bodies, I have clients practice watching their breathing and their pulse or heartbeat. It's not far from here to watching thoughts as they come along. Practicing this a little bit every day makes mindfulness something that is more available to us when we need it, whether we're experiencing anxiety and obsessive thoughts or just wanting to connect more fully with valued moments in our lives. What this practicing looks like varies widely. For some people it's sitting quietly and meditating, but for others it's taking a walk, enjoying a cup of tea, working in the garden, or preparing a simple meal in a mindful way.

Listen, Look, Smell, Feel, Taste…

"Oh no…" you may ask, "do we need to move through all of the senses now?" Well…it might not be a bad idea. The problem with obsessive thinking is that it constantly pulls us away from our senses. Even when our senses are involved in our obsessions, like Anthony's heightened awareness of the look or smell of poo, the focus of the obsession is on our memories, judgments, and narratives about these sensory experiences. In other words, our thoughts. We will come to observing our thoughts later in this chapter, but for now, let's start with something that offers some ballast to help us with that: observing what we hear, see, smell, feel, and taste, independent of our judgments about those experiences. Our senses bring us a continual newsfeed of information about the present moment, most of which we ignore as we go about our day. Because the sounds we can hear, the colors and shapes we can see, and what we can smell, feel, or taste is limited to our experience of the current moment, there is an immediacy to sensation that can be very grounding. A good first step toward being more mindful is to simply attend very closely to what our senses are offering us in the present moment. You can think of this as more fully contacting and "staying with" your experience.

Other than when we are intentionally practicing being mindful, one of the most common reasons for bringing attention to our sensory experiences is to evaluate or judge them. This is what happens when we go to a new restaurant, or eat some dish we've never tasted before. It's what happens when we're shopping for new sheets and feel how soft or scratchy they are. It may be the way we look at art in a museum, or how we use our nose to see if we can get one more day out of that dirty shirt. It's often the goal of evaluating an experience and judging it to be either "good" or "bad" that brings our focus to it, and to our senses. This is what makes the difference between "wine tasting" and wine drinking. When we are practicing mindfulness, we want to bring this same level of attention and presence to our experience, but without an investment in the evaluations and judgments that tend to come with that increased focus. We immerse ourselves in the experience solely for the sake of more fully experiencing it. As we do this, judgments will indeed arise. When they do, we can experience them in a defused way, as just another part of our experience. A judgment is not a part of the thing that is being judged. It's more like a byproduct of our interaction with the world. When you practice mindfulness, allow yourself to have the judgment without fully buying it. One way to do this is to label these thoughts as "judgments," observing them the same way you observe a color or a smell.

Start by listening. When you get to the end of this paragraph, take a few minutes to sit and really listen. Close your eyes and focus on all that you're able to hear. If you're indoors, start by listening to the sounds you can hear in the room you're in. Is there a clock ticking? A fan running? What about you? Can you hear yourself running? Can you hear your breath as it comes and goes? Perhaps a gurgling from your belly? There may be a hum or a ringing sound, which is the way many of us hear silence. Now listen for sounds coming from other rooms and from outdoors. When you notice yourself thinking about what made the noise, or why it sounds that way, notice these thoughts, then bring your attention back to the sound itself, staying with it. Notice the separation of yourself as listener, or context, and the sounds you are hearing, which are all content. Try it now.

Looking is something that we do all day long, as long as our eyes are open. Seeing is something that happens less often. When it does, it is often a means to an end. We see where we are going, what we are doing, or what others are doing. We are focused, not on what we see, but on the meaning of what we see. You're doing it right now as you see these words. Mindful seeing is seeing as an end in itself. I think of this kind of seeing as experientially *absorbing* what we see. This concept helps me to stay more closely attuned to what I am seeing, allowing myself to steep in the experience. Seeing color is a good place to begin. Start with the color yellow, since it's a little less common and tends to jump out at us. Wherever you are right now, take a couple of minutes to carefully look around and really *see* everything in your field of vision that is yellow. Imagine that you are soaking up as much of the color yellow as you can get. Notice any variations in shade or saturation. Notice any thoughts, associations, or emotions that arise, then gently bring your focus back to the yellowness itself. Try it now. When you're done, try the same thing with the color blue. Notice what a different experience it is to see blue. Yellow is one thing, and blue is another thing entirely. Try it now. Now do it again, but this time try to see and sit with the shape and texture of everything you see that is yellow, and then everything that is blue. Notice that you can see the texture and contours of things as well as their color, "touching" them with your eyes. This is mindful seeing. This is a wonderful way to see the world when you take a walk.

For most mammals, the sense of smell is primary. My little cat is constantly sniffing things. Whether it's a package that has just been delivered, a jacket hung over the back of a chair, or the hand that's petting her, she uses her nose to make sense of things and where they fit into her world. Humans tend to ignore or avoid smells, often covering them up with grooming and cleaning products, cutting ourselves off from a rich source of information about people and places. Food is one exception. We rely on smells when preparing food and to tell us when to eat something or throw it out. Smells can bring us into the present moment, but they can also transport us, bringing up powerful memories of the past. Being mindful of smells means noticing these memories and reactions as part of our experience, even as we allow our awareness to rest more fully in the smell itself. Closing your eyes, try smelling your fingertips, then the palm of your hand. Now smell the back of your hand. Notice the subtle differences. Smell your clothing. Can you smell laundry soap? Toiletries? Sweat? Next time you're in the kitchen, try closing your eyes and smelling the room. Now try smelling the bathroom, then the bedroom. Notice that it's possible to identify a room just by its smell. This is mindful smelling.

Your skin is covered with touch receptors. These sensors quickly habituate to constant pressure so that you're less aware of things like the clothes on your back, the shoes on your feet, or the seat of a chair pressing against your butt. Your fingertips, however, are jam-packed with sensors and offer you a constant feast of intense, rich, nuanced sensations. You lead with your fingertips to discover whether the water coming from the tap is hot or cold, whether the counter is wet or dry, and whether or not it's a good idea to take that seat on the subway. A big part of the experience of eating has to do with the texture of foods. We touch the food with our tongue as we taste it. We note the change in texture as we chew, and we use this information to determine when to swallow. With your eyes closed, notice the vast variety of what you can feel where you are sitting right now. Start with your fingertips, feeling the crisp pages of this book, or the coolness of the device you're reading it on. Touch the chair you're sitting in. Let your fingertips explore your own clothing, your skin, your hair. Now notice what you can feel with the rest of your body. Can you feel where your skin makes contact with your clothing? Can you feel the pressure of the furniture that's supporting you? Can you feel the inside of your mouth? Move your tongue around, feeling the roof of your mouth, and the surface of your teeth. As you breathe in and out, can you feel the air moving past the skin of your nostrils? This is mindful touch.

The best way to explore the sense of taste is by eating or drinking slowly and luxuriantly. To isolate the experience of taste, it helps to stop chewing, allowing food to sit on your tongue and melt in your mouth. The taste buds are highly specialized. Some are more sensitive to sweetness, others to bitterness. Still others are specifically attuned to saltiness or sourness. We experience these tastes more or less with different areas of the tongue. Try moving food from one area of the tongue to another. One of my favorite things to eat mindfully is dry cereal. I like it for the texture as much as for the taste. Some cereals are light and flaky, others are hard and rough. If you hold cereal in your mouth without chewing, some cereals will soften up right away, while others take a long time to turn to mush. Often, one side of a piece of cereal will feel and taste different from the other side. When you bite into it, cereal tends to make a satisfying crunching sound that you can hear inside of your head. It goes down easy and leaves an aftertaste of grains and sugars. Notice that there's more going on here than taste. Eating involves all of the senses, from the way the food looks and smells to the texture, the taste, and even the sounds that it makes.

A Symphony of Senses

Much of our daily experience involves this complex blending of different senses. Eating is a favorite example, but others include doing the laundry, taking a bath or shower, and mailing a letter. We can think of these experiences as including layers of sensation. When we practice mindfulness, our awareness can flow gently from one aspect of our experience to another. We focus on the warmth of the bath water on our skin, then we notice the scent of the bubble bath, then hear the drip, drip of water from the tap. It's also possible, however, for us to notice and attend to more than one layer of our experience at the same time. It's a bit like listening to an orchestra. If we choose to, we can focus more on the higher-pitched melody of the wind instruments. Or, we can tune into and tap our foot to the lower, underlying beat of the bass notes, following the rhythm. When we are listening with the most openness to our experience, however, we are hearing all of the instruments together, allowing ourselves to be carried along by the whole, multilayered experience of the music. When we listen, look, smell, feel, or taste mindfully, we can notice not only complex sensory experience, but an emotional and thinking layer of experience as well. Observing this from the perspective of self-as-context, all of this is content. When we experience it with willingness and openness as part of the present moment, we begin to see that it is transitory and separate from the more enduring entity that is *us*, the contextual self.

Going for a Walk

One of the most accessible, healthy ways to practice mindfulness is by going for a walk. Walking, whether in an animated, noisy urban environment or in a placid, natural setting, provides a rich, varied, and slowly shifting flow of sensory experience. It offers the opportunity to repeatedly bring ourselves into the moment, seeing, hearing, smelling, touching, and absorbing the world as we move through it. Taking a fairly long walk allows time for the chatter of our minds to quiet down and for our awareness to come more fully into harmony with our surroundings.

There's no ideal place to practice mindful walking. Don't worry so much about finding a quiet place. Mindfulness is about meeting your experience and attending to it. Some people actually find this easier to do when there is more activity to focus on. Try mixing it up. I enjoy mindful walks through the bustling heart of San Francisco's business district as well as in the quietest and greenest parts of Golden Gate Park. Remember, mindfulness is about cultivating a special relationship with your experience. This doesn't mean finding the "right" experience. Rather, it's about being open to and connected with whatever experience you're having in a given moment. The first few times you try this, it helps to plan your route ahead of time. That way, you won't be distracted by thoughts of where to go next. Later, you might decide to let your mind choose the route as you walk, and to watch it making these small decisions.

Before starting the mindful part of your walk, it can help to close your eyes for a moment and get in touch with the experience of being in your body. Notice your breathing as it comes and goes, be aware of your posture, and just feel your body as a physical fact, the vehicle that will carry you through the world. Before opening your eyes, allow your immediate environment to seep into your awareness. Make contact with where you are by listening to the sounds of that environment. Whether it's the songs of birds or the honking of car horns, these are the sounds of the living, noisy world. Invite them in with openness. Feel the wind on your skin. As you breathe in, notice the smell of the place. You are here, now. When you're ready to meet the rest of this experience, open your eyes... slowly. Don't look around too much at first. Just open your eyes and pay attention to what you see. Notice the colors, the shapes, the texture. Notice movement. Just soak it up for a few minutes. Don't forget to notice the sounds and to feel the breeze. This is the world. You're here. Now.

You'll also notice thoughts about all of this. Thoughts about what you are seeing, the name of that tree, the advertising on the side of that truck, what's that sound?... the chattering of your mind as it sorts, labels, and organizes your experience. Let your mind do its thing, just noticing it the same way you notice the birds singing or the horns honking. Your job is to see, to listen, to feel, to soak it all up. You will probably have thoughts about yourself. Am I doing this right? Are people looking at me? Is it okay to pass gas? Notice these thoughts as more singing and honking, just another layer of your experience. Bring your attention back to the world. To help with this, look around a bit. Bring in more information, more experience. The novelty and variety will help you to stay with the whole experience instead of being carried away from it by the chatter of your mind.

At first, being and staying mindful is easier if you walk slowly. Just looking...and looking...and looking. It's also okay to touch things, to stop and close your eyes again, to listen, to feel the breeze. Slowly pick up the pace. As you move, try to see as much as you can. When you notice yourself leaving the moment, thinking back to yesterday, or years ago, or looking forward in time, just gently bring your focus back to now. Pay attention to the movement of the leaves on the trees or the flow of traffic. Notice that these things are real and here. Your thoughts are real also, but not in the same way. The times, places, and people of your thoughts are not here. Not real in the same way as the world you are walking through. It's natural for the mind to wander away from the present moment. It's like a puppy that way, all over the place. Let it wander a bit, but then gently guide it back. Bring it back to the present moment with compassion and an acceptance of its wandering nature. Don't slap the puppy. Your mind is part of your experience, like everything else. Just doing its thing.

At first, try being mindful for about twenty minutes during your walk. You can walk a bit before and for a while after this twenty minutes, just for the exercise, but bring your intention and focus to mindful walking for a set period. With practice, see if you can expand this period of increased mindfulness to thirty minutes, then forty-five minutes. Eventually, on longer walks, you may notice that you slide gently in and out of mindfulness throughout the walk. This is fine. The goal is to be more mindful for more of the time that you are walking, not to be all-mindful all the time. If you notice that you're getting caught up in heavy thinking about things other than the walk, having intense dialogues with people who aren't present, planning or problem solving, or maybe just worrying about things, stop for a moment, close your eyes, take a few breaths, and begin again.

Watching Your Body, Breath, and Mind

Mindful walking is about being more fully in the world, and letting the world exist more fully in your experience. Another way to practice mindfulness is to sit quietly and observe the more immediate, intimate world of your body, your breathing, and your thoughts. Start by finding a comfortable spot...but not too comfortable. Remember, this is about paying attention. You want to be relaxed but alert. Sitting up is much better than lying down.

The Body Scan

Close your eyes, and notice what your body feels like. Start by doing a slow scan of your body, starting with your toes and working your way up. Just notice your toes. Start with the left foot, if you like. Notice what your toes feel like. It's okay to move them a little. Now the other foot. Then notice the balls of your feet. You can notice both feet at once or take on one at a time. There's no one correct way to do this. Now notice the arches and the heels of your feet. Notice your ankles, your lower legs, your upper legs. Notice where your butt makes contact with the chair. Notice your back, lower, middle, and upper. Observe the positions of your arms. Notice your hands; what are they touching? Now be aware of your neck, and then your head. Notice your scalp, and the muscles of your face. When you're done with this, notice your body as a whole. See if you can experience your body as a physical object, with mass and weight. Notice your body at rest, supported by the chair you are sitting in.

This is a body scan. It is a simple, brief way to practice mindfulness by bringing your awareness more fully to your body as it exists in the present moment. The goal is not to relax your body, though doing a body scan can be very relaxing. If you notice areas of tension or discomfort in your body, simply observe this, making room for it as part of your experience, noticing any thoughts or judgments that you have about it, and then continue with your scan. When you first try the body scan, take your time. Start by giving yourself a good fifteen or twenty minutes to move from your toes up to your head. As you get more practiced, you'll be able to complete the scan more quickly. When you're able to do it in about five minutes, you can use it as step one of a three-step process. Once you are more fully in your body, the second step is to notice and attend to your breathing.

Watching Your Breathing

After completing the body scan, with your eyes still closed, watch yourself breathing in and out. Notice that your body knows just how to do this. Don't worry about whether you're breathing the right or wrong way for this. Remember, you've been breathing practically your whole life; just notice it. Notice the movement of air past your nostrils as you breathe in. See if you can feel the air moving past the back of your eyes, through your sinuses, and past the back of your throat with each breath. You may feel your chest expanding as you breathe, or feel the breath all the way down in your belly. Watch this ongoing, complex process the way you might watch a machine operating. Notice that breathing is a process that continues, on and on, whether you're watching it or not.

Next, find the one spot in your body where you are *most aware* of your breath as it comes and goes. This will be a different spot for different people. It may even change for you over time. Just find the spot, or pick a spot at random, and let your attention settle gently on that spot...like a butterfly alighting on a flower. Let your attention focus on this spot as you observe your breath coming and going. Notice that it's possible for you to observe only one breath at a time: the current one. It's impossible to observe the breath you had a minute ago, or the breath you'll be taking after this one. It's only possible to observe *this breath,* in *this moment.* And, now...*this* breath...in *this* moment. Let each breath act as an anchor, connecting you to its corresponding moment, so that watching your breathing, in and out, holds you, gently, in the present. Practice this a bit. When you're able to stay with your breath for a good ten minutes or so, without being carried away from it by the stream of consciousness, you're ready to add on the third and final step: watching your thoughts the same way you've been watching your breathing.

Watching Your Thoughts

Watching your thoughts in a mindful way means observing the thoughts without being carried off by them. Watching your breathing for a bit first is a good way to get a sense of what this is like. Your breathing is an ongoing process, just like thinking. When you observe your breathing, you do so from a fixed perspective of consciousness. This means that you stay in one place, observing each breath as it comes and goes. You can watch your thoughts from this same fixed perspective. The thoughts come and go while you stay put.

It's a little like sitting on a bench in a subway or train station and watching the trains come and go. A train pulls up to the platform, you notice what type of train it is and where it's headed. You watch it leave, and wait for the next train to show up. This one's an express train; that one's a local. This one's going to the airport; that one's going to Vienna. This train is crowded with passengers; that one is completely empty. The people on this train seem to be laughing at you. Everyone on the next one looks really sad. Sometimes, when we're watching our thoughts come and go in this way, we accidentally board one of the trains. The doors close behind us, and we're off. One of our thoughts has carried us away. We find ourselves on a journey, temporarily in another time and place, doing, planning, talking, remembering, struggling. When you notice that this has happened, don't panic. Just get off the train at the next station. Bring your attention back to your breathing for a minute or two. Watching your breath come and go helps you to reconnect with that fixed perspective of consciousness; it helps you to settle onto another bench. When the next train comes by, use the awareness of your breath to keep yourself on the bench. Notice the train, notice where it's headed, and let it go. You may notice a lot of trains that are headed for The Obsession Loop. This shouldn't be surprising. Treat these the same way you treat all the other trains, the ones marked "Next Meal" or "Itchy Nose." Another common train is the "You're Doing This Wrong" train or the "You Call THIS Mindfulness?" express. Smile at these, and let them go. Wait for the next one...here it comes. Try using this visual metaphor of watching trains come and go as you practice watching your thoughts. You may want to try it now.

I find that when I'm watching my thoughts in this manner, after a while they seem to come and go with a certain rhythm, much like my breathing or my heartbeat. Getting a feel for this rhythm can help you to stay on the platform as well. Anticipating the next train helps you to let go of the one that's just leaving the station. Another way to experience thoughts in this rhythmic way is to imagine them as being projected on a screen, as a slide show. The thing about a slide show is that the slides come one after another. With an old-fashioned mechanical slide projector, the screen goes dark for a moment between each slide, and there's an audible "click." This tells us "Here comes the next slide..." I find that this rhythm helps me to let go of the previous slide in anticipation of the next one. It's different from watching a movie. A movie is fluid and continuous. It flows and carries us along. This is often how we experience thoughts. Watching trains or slides coming and going makes it easier to experience yourself as observing them from one spot. Here's my thought as an image or words on a screen, "click," here's the next thought, "click," another thought comes along, "click," more thoughts.

Yet another way to imagine this procession of thoughts is to imagine them moving past on a conveyor belt. You're Lucy or Ethel working at the chocolate factory. The thoughts come by on the conveyor belt, one after the other, like chocolates. Except, instead of trying to process or package them, and instead of stuffing them into your mouth, you just let them go by. Your mind is a thought machine, and it has an endless supply of thoughts; the conveyor belt just runs and runs. No need to try to keep up, and no need to climb onto the belt. Remember the sushi boats? You're having thoughts. No need to buy any of them.

Finally, a more traditional metaphor that comes from the Buddhist tradition is to imagine yourself relaxing beside a river or a stream. Here, watching your breathing is like watching the continuous movement of the water as it flows past you. When you notice a thought, imagine it floating past on the water, like a leaf or a twig. Let each thought be carried away by the current, then notice the next one to come along. If you lose your fixed perspective, noticing that you have fallen into the river and are being carried along by the current, just climb back onto the shore, find another comfortable spot, and resume your mindful watching of the flowing water. I suppose this metaphor has the advantage of being a bit more organic than trains, slides, and conveyor belts. Experiment with all of these, or find your own way of watching your thoughts. Some people see them as clouds drifting by in a blue sky. I know a financial analyst who likes to watch his thoughts scroll by on an electronic stock ticker.

Be patient as you feel your way into this process of sitting quietly, observing your body, observing your breathing, observing your thoughts, observing your experience without getting carried away from the here and now. Try to make time to practice this on a regular basis. For some people the morning is a good time. Twenty minutes over a mindfully sipped cup of coffee to set the tone for the day. For others, the end of the day is a better time, as part of the transition from working to being present at home. If every day seems like too much, try doing it two or three days of the week. It might help to pick a specific spot. It definitely helps to pick a specific time. If you can't find twenty minutes, ten minutes will do. If you need a name for this activity, you can call it "just sitting." Some people call it mindful sitting. Many people call it meditation.

Practicing Mindfulness

Whether you practice mindfulness by sitting and watching your thoughts, by doing the occasional body scan, or by walking, know that what you are doing in these moments is just that...practicing. You are developing mindfulness as a skill. You're practicing mindfulness to get better at it so that you can apply this skill when you think it might help you to live a better life. Aside from these more formal ways to practice mindfulness, there are countless moments for developing mindfulness as you go about your day. Eating a meal or snack, washing dishes, and brushing and flossing your teeth are all excellent opportunities for focusing and being in the moment. Exercising, listening to music, spending time with pets, and engaging in hobbies like knitting or gardening all invite us to be more present, developing and strengthening our "mindfulness muscles."

When you find yourself struggling with an obsessive thought, taking a moment to observe your breathing and then observe the thought in a mindful way can help you to let go of the struggle. It can help you to make room for the thought, to coexist with your experience. Noticing all that you are aware of in the current moment makes the obsessive thought part of a larger experience. A mindful perspective on obsessive thoughts can make it easier to say no to compulsive behaviors, instead committing to a course of action that holds more value for you than temporary relief from a thought. The next chapter will focus on clarifying which choices bring the most value into your life. What do *you*, as an individual, value most in life? What is the best use of your time and energy? If you're not making choices based on obsessive thoughts and fear, how will you decide what to do? If you are not your thoughts and feelings, who are you?

CHAPTER 10

The Compass and the Barometer

When Anthony and I were working on his contamination obsessions, there was a motto I heard from him over and over. It went something like this: "I don't ask for much. I just want to live my life and do my thing." With some prompting, Anthony explained what he meant by this. As he saw it, he had a simple but almost ideal life. He had a stable but undemanding job that allowed him lots of time for running and for mixing music, his two passions in life. He lived alone in a rent-controlled one-bedroom apartment, which he was able to maintain exactly as he saw fit. His life had been this way for years, and his focus was on maintaining it, exactly as it was. He was mostly successful in this, and yet, for one reason or another, he always seemed to be slightly less than happy. Just when things were moving along smoothly, something always seemed to happen to throw things off. There were small but constant challenges thrown in his path. He was constantly having to "cross the street because of someone else's shit." To Anthony, this seemed true both literally and figuratively. The sneezed-on jacket is a good example. Here he had finally found the perfect jacket, and some old guy comes along and sneezes all over it. Running shoes were another problem. Anthony had a very hard time finding running shoes that fit just right. When he did, he always bought several pairs. That way, if he found something suspicious stuck in his treads and had to throw a pair out, he had an immediate backup available. The problem was that specific shoe models were constantly being changed and discontinued. Anthony just wanted things clean and tidy and to stay exactly the same. Was that too much to ask?

Anthony had been dating Lisa for several years. He loved her very much and often described her as "the perfect girlfriend." Lisa accepted Anthony's quirks and knew how he liked things. For example, she was the only person he allowed into his apartment. "I don't even mind her using my bathroom, because she's always really careful about stuff, and keeps things clean." As far as Anthony was concerned, this could have continued indefinitely, but for the fact that Lisa suddenly wanted to change everything. When her roommate got engaged and asked Lisa to move out, she decided that it might be a good time for her and Anthony to move in together. She was open to moving into his place or pooling their resources and looking for a larger apartment together. Anthony was thrown into a tailspin by both of these suggestions. "I love having Lisa around, but both of my closets are completely full. I don't know where she thinks she would put her things." As far as finding a bigger place, this also seemed unthinkable. "I love my apartment, and I'll never get such a good deal on rent anywhere else." For Anthony, it was hard to see why Lisa couldn't just make some other arrangement that would not require him to disrupt the near perfection and relative stability of his single-occupancy life. Lisa, on the other hand, felt that sharing a space was the logical next step toward sharing a life together. From her perspective, if they couldn't make some move in that direction, the relationship was likely to come to an end. The idea of breaking up was even more upsetting to Anthony than the suggestion that Lisa move in. "We can't break up. She's the perfect girlfriend for me! I don't want to have to start going on *dates*...are you kidding?!"

For Anthony, the question we needed to answer when he was faced with this dilemma was not whether it would be uncomfortable or hard for him to move in with Lisa, but whether it would be worth it. Did his inclination to keep his life exactly the same, year after year, and to avoid sharing it more fully with Lisa indicate that he valued living a single life more than a shared one? Or was this more of a response to his fear of change and of giving up control? Would the choice to continue living alone be a move *toward* something he really wanted, or a move *away* from something that made him anxious? This is the difference between being guided by values and being guided by fear. When we pursue our values, the movement is forward, even though the path may be difficult and frightening. When our choices are governed by fear, the movement tends to be backward or side-to-side and circular, depending on what is less uncomfortable. The goal is often to stay in one place, like treading water.

It can be just as much work as moving toward something, but with a very different outcome. This is when therapy that focuses on exploring your *feelings* is less than helpful. Anthony already knew a lot about his fears. It was clear to him that having Lisa move in was more frightening than keeping things the same. What was less clear is what he valued more: a spotless bathroom and enough closet space to quarantine contaminated clothing, or Lisa's love and companionship. The anxiety and all the efforts directed at avoiding it had obscured Anthony's sense of what he really cared about. When he thought about moving toward a shared life with Lisa, there was so much anxiety blocking his path that it seemed pointless to talk about whether or not he wanted that.

Anxiety and Purpose

Over three decades of talking with people about their anxiety, I've found that the experience of anxiety itself is very similar from person to person. What is unique and varies greatly is the way people respond to anxiety, and why those responses are problematic for them. While anxiety is certainly uncomfortable, the real costs lie in the efforts to control and avoid it. Social isolation, substance abuse, missed personal and professional opportunities, and a massive expenditure of time and energy are among the legacies of years spent avoiding uncomfortable feelings. Most patients who seek treatment for OCD and other anxiety disorders are aware to varying degrees of these costs and are ready to make some changes. Others seem to see therapy as just another temporary respite from the discomfort, a balm for painful feelings. While empathy and support are an important part of any therapy, when it's limited to that, seeing a therapist can easily become one more facet of a complex regimen of avoidance and comfort seeking. When we discuss the possibility of taking on some of the things they have been avoiding, or giving up some of their compulsive behaviors, these comfort-seeking patients often respond with some version of "Why on Earth would I do that?" Why would they intentionally choose to do something that they know will make them uncomfortable? To the extent that they have found ways of getting by within the constraints that anxiety has set for them, why would they rock the boat? For what purpose? For many of these patients, years of avoiding painful feelings has led them to forget that they ever wanted more out of life than avoiding pain. Instead of moving toward what they value, hope for, and dream of, their path is made up of moves away from what they dread, worry about, and fear. Does any of this sound familiar?

The fact that you are reading this book suggests some honest measurement of the costs of avoiding triggers and performing compulsions. However, it's not unusual to minimize exactly how much you have given up. We often downplay the value of those things that it would be difficult to strive toward. In Aesop's fable *The Fox and the Grapes*, when the hungry fox finds a tempting cluster of grapes too high for him to reach, he decides that they are probably sour anyway. The costs of avoidance can be particularly insidious. We might tell ourselves that we are indeed pursuing richer, closer relationships or reaching for creative or professional goals, but then hold back in subtle ways out of fear. Keeping personal interactions superficial, sticking with what is familiar and safe, and limiting the scope of our aspirations are all ways of catering to anxiety at the expense of what we value. Over time, we lose our sense of purpose or direction. The cumulative effect of this subtle avoidance is less of what we value in life and, ironically, just as much or more anxiety. When our orientation is toward protecting what we have and avoiding risk, we are living in fear. When our choices are guided by what we value and who we aspire to be, even though we may feel fear, we are living in hope.

Plotting Your Course

One way to think about life decisions like the one Anthony faced is to imagine that we are sailing in open waters. If we are going to get anywhere in particular, we have to choose a direction and plot a course that moves us in that direction. On a boat, the instrument that points us in any direction is a compass. The compass is a reliable guide because of its stability. North is always north, East is east, South is south, West is west. The compass lets us know when we are on or off course. Our values are like a compass for our lives. An awareness of the things, people, and experiences that make life more valuable to us can guide us in our choices, moving us in a particular direction, toward a life of increasing value. Values are unique to each individual. What I value may not be what you value. Within a given individual, however, values are quite stable. They may change gradually over the course of a lifetime, but from day to day, they remain largely the same. North is north, East is east.

The other instrument on board our ship is a barometer. The barometer lets us know what the weather is like wherever we happen to be. It can forecast things like choppy waters and headwinds. It can help us to avoid stormy seas and find smooth sailing. What it doesn't tell us is where we're going. Our feelings, especially feelings like anxiety, are like a barometer. Anxiety suggests to us that the waters ahead may be difficult. Choosing to move forward through choppy waters means being willing to feel discomfort, or even pain. Sometimes, based on what the barometer tells us, we change course. We steer to the right or to the left, avoiding the worst of the storm. We point our ship toward calmer waters. Sometimes this works. As long as we use the compass to correct our course, it's not always necessary to sail through the worst part of the storm. The problem comes when we begin to steer our ship mostly by the barometer. When we consistently avoid rough weather and plot a course based on where the waters are quietest, we find ourselves without direction, and we end up in no place in particular. Feelings are important. They often give us useful information. But, like the barometer, they aren't so useful as guides for our direction in life. Anthony had been steering his ship by the barometer of his anxiety for so long, he had completely lost track of his compass. He had forgotten to ask himself what he cared about and what he wanted to get out of his time on the planet. Because its role is so specialized, the anxious mind does not concern itself with these questions. Fortunately, there is much more to who we are than our anxious thoughts and feelings.

Values and the Contextual Self

Our thoughts and feelings, like all the content of our experience, tend to flow and change constantly. Our sense of what is valuable, on the other hand, is more enduring and stable. Our values offer a perspective from which to view our experiences, a fixed frame for our shifting thoughts and feelings. This consistency and stability are qualities that our values share with the larger, enduring perspective on the world that is our contextual self. Getting in touch with our values can remind us of who we really are. It puts us in touch with the enduring, larger self for whom fear and anxious thoughts are fleeting experiential content. When you're ninety-five years old, looking back on the life you've led, how likely is it that you will remember what you were thinking or feeling today? Isn't it more likely that you will remember what you did? The experiences and relationships you had? If your choices have been guided by your values rather than reactions to your thoughts and feelings, don't you think you'll be more likely to see a pattern that more accurately reflects who you really are?

For Anthony, the dilemma of whether to move forward into a more intimately entwined, committed relationship with Lisa offered an opportunity to connect more fully with his larger self. It raised questions of who he was and who he wished to be. It was a reminder that there was much more to Anthony as a person than his fear of snot and shit. He captured the distinction between his true self and his fears very clearly when he said, "I want to make my life bigger, but the OCD wants to keep it small." Whether he thought about it or not, Anthony had a distinct set of values. He was extremely creative and, in many ways, socially engaged. He loved music and its ability to capture emotion and bring people together. He lived these values by mixing music and performing as a guest DJ at various venues around the city. In these settings, he could be very outgoing, and he had become well connected within the city's artistic community. A deep thinker and a keen observer of people, Anthony had a sharp sense of humor and an appreciation of irony. While he could be a bit rigid about diet and exercise, this reflected a clear value of and commitment to physical fitness and good health. Though not particularly motivated by money, he cared about financial security and was a good saver and a skilled investor. Anthony deeply loved and appreciated the person that Lisa was. He consistently looked forward to the time he spent with her and made a concerted effort to be attentive to her needs. In most ways, he was a very good boyfriend. Like most people, Anthony *had* a compass on board, and he made use of it... until he didn't.

The problem was the barometer. The feeling part of Anthony's experience included a very loud snot and shit alarm. When this alarm was going off, it was so loud that he forgot to look at his compass, and sometimes forgot that it existed. When his contamination fears were triggered, Anthony tended to react by steering clear of anything that involved uncomfortable thoughts and feelings. Doing this over and over again from day to day had taken him very far off course. Anthony's cleaning and grooming rituals sometimes made him late for club engagements and had prevented him from landing a regular gig. Part of what kept him at the same day job for so many years was the flexibility of his schedule, which allowed for extra time showering and cleaning up when he felt it was called for. While he enjoyed meeting new people and had a personality that others were drawn to, Anthony's anxiety could make it hard for him to develop and maintain deeper friendships. He refused many invitations because his fear of stepping on something gross or dirty made it difficult for him to navigate city sidewalks while having a conversation. Socializing at home was not an option because he was afraid that others would contaminate his clean apartment with their dirty clothes and shoes. Anthony tended to minimize the cumulative costs of all of these small avoidance maneuvers. Now, while he clearly valued and wanted to hold onto and nurture his relationship with Lisa, his fear had him steering in the opposite direction.

Fears Disguised as Values

Sometimes it can be difficult to tell what is a value and what is a fear. When Anthony and I talked about what prevented him from having people over, he sometimes described it as a value-driven choice. He said things like "I value my privacy" and "I enjoy spending time alone." Both of these statements were true, but these values were not what was driving his choice to not let friends cross his threshold. While he did value privacy and time alone, he also valued connection and companionship. It's not unusual to have competing values that pull us in opposing directions. When this happens, people commonly try to strike a balance, steering a course that honors both values to some degree. If alone time is north and party time is east, we sail northeast. Sometimes our fear and our values both suggest a move in the same direction, but fear tends to point us more strongly toward absolutes, sending us due north, when a value-guided course would be more northeast. For example, Anthony valued fitness and exercise, which led him to run most days. His need to maintain a consistent, orderly schedule made him inflexible when social opportunities conflicted with his running schedule. Instead of running a bit earlier or later in the day (northeast), he passed on activities that he might otherwise have enjoyed in order to stick to his running schedule (due north). Similarly, his obsession with finding the "right" running shoes and keeping them clean was not exactly a clear reflection of his fitness values. The anxiety about his shoes often threw him (literally) off course in the pursuit of his values-driven fitness goals.

The Values Test

One reason that it's easy to confuse fears with values is that they both reside inside of us. When they are pulling us in clearly opposing directions, it can be a little easier to distinguish them. When they seem to pull us in similar directions, it can be harder to tell them apart based on our outside choices. In these moments, it can help to notice what our experiences of valuing and of fearing are like on the inside. Here is a simple exercise that many of my patients find helpful. I call it the Values Test.

Sit quietly with your eyes closed. Just watch your breathing for a moment and get settled into your body, noticing and getting in touch with your physical self. When you're ready, think of something you're afraid of. It can be big or small, but bring to mind something that makes you anxious or uncomfortable or that you worry about. Try to open yourself up to feeling the anxiety in your body. When you feel it, try to notice exactly where in your body the anxiety resides. If you could draw a line around the anxiety, where would you draw it?

Next, think about something or someone you value and care about. It can be anything about the world or about life that you value, a relationship with a specific person or group of people, a favorite activity or an intellectual pursuit. Don't be distracted by fears you may have related to this value. Just try to focus on the valuing, caring, or loving itself. Feel the value this thing, person, or activity holds for you. When you are in touch with that, notice where in your body you experience the valuing. Can you draw a line or circle around it the same way you did with the anxiety?

What did you notice about the two parts of this exercise? Did you experience anxiety and valuing in different ways? When it came to localizing and drawing a line around the experience, was this easier to do with the anxiety or with your sense of valuing? Did you experience them in the same part of your body or in different locations? I've walked patients through this exercise hundreds of times over the years, and most of them report a similar experience. Almost without exception, they report that, compared to valuing, anxiety is easier to locate in a specific, discrete part of their body. It has clearer limits and boundaries. It's easier to draw a clear circle around the anxiety. When it comes to the second part of the exercise, their experience of valuing and caring is more diffuse and harder to locate physically. Many people say that they experience valuing as being everywhere. Others say that it's lower down in their body than the anxiety, or deeper within them. In any case, almost everyone is able to tell the difference, when they pay attention, between fearing something and valuing something. You can think of the Values Test as both a way of identifying what is coming from your barometer and a way of getting in touch with your compass. With practice, it will become easier to tell the difference.

What Values Are Not

I tend to tread carefully when discussing values with patients. In fact, I often avoid using the actual word "values" at first, instead talking with patients about "purpose," what they "care about," and what qualities and experiences "add value" to their life. I've learned to do this because the word "values" has been used many different ways and picked up a number of confusing connotations. From an ACT perspective, your values are simply whatever makes life valuable to you. Before exploring this further, it may be helpful to clarify what values are not.

Feelings

We've already talked about mistaking fear for values, but there is often a more general confusion between our feelings about people and things and our values related to them. A helpful distinction to make is that feelings tend to come and go, while values persist. For example, you may value and want to keep your job. How you *feel* about your job, however, likely varies from day to day. Do you only show up for work on the days when you feel enthusiastic about it? Showing up for work even on days when you're not that into it is living your values. This is the "commitment" in acceptance and commitment therapy.

Close relationships are another example. Think about a person you are close to and care about. If you spend time with this person and put effort into interacting with them in a nice way, it likely reflects the degree to which you value that relationship. Now think about your feelings for and about this person. Are they consistently the same, or do they tend to fluctuate and shift? What if you only made an effort to interact with and be nice to this person when you were feeling really positive about them? How well would that work? Commitment to a relationship means that we work on it even as our feelings toward the person shift from love to annoyance to anger, and back to love again. Commitment is about acting on our values, proceeding consistently in a valued direction, independent of day-to-day shifts in how we are feeling. In this way, our values help us to coordinate and direct our choices over the long term. This is how we develop and nurture a life that we value even as we experience things like anxiety, ambivalence, and uncertainty.

Morals or Rules

People sometimes use the word "values" as another word for morals or rules for living a good life. This is the meaning implied by "family values," "small town values," or even "San Francisco values." As it's used here and in ACT, the word "values" does not refer to any set of rules or code of conduct imposed from the outside. Rather, it refers to your own unique and internal sense of what makes life good. While values give your life direction and can point you toward specific choices, they are not fixed rules about how to behave. Holding a particular value guides us, but it does not direct or control us. While we may set verbal rules for ourselves based on our values, the rule and the value behind it are two different things. Living our values sometimes requires a flexibility that is inconsistent with rigid rules. For example, while running regularly was an expression of Anthony's fitness values, running at the same time every day, even when it meant not seeing friends, amounted to following a rule that moved him away from his value of nurturing friendships. When it comes to living your values, *guidelines* are often more helpful than rules.

Goals

There is sometimes a similar disconnect between our values and the goals that we set related to those values. Setting goals that move us in a valued direction can be extremely helpful, but it's important to remember that values and goals are not the same thing. Values point us in a particular direction, while goals are specific destinations that lie in that direction. Often, making real progress in a valued direction requires being flexible about our goals. Think about the elected official who *values* serving others and making the world a better place. To continue doing this, she sets the *goal* of getting re-elected. How often have we seen politicians betraying their core values in the pursuit of this goal? I often work with patients who have latched onto a specific professional goal that ends up moving their lives away from the very values that brought them to their profession in the first place.

People who pursue the same goal often do so because of different values. Think of the politician again. Have you known people to run for office because of values other than serving others and making the world a better place? Likewise, even a goal as simple as playing golf can be an expression of a range of different values for different people. For some, the value is taking their golfing skills to the highest level possible. For others, golfing is an opportunity to be outdoors or to focus on something in a mindful way. While some people may value golfing as a way to network professionally, others value it as a way to maintain connections with family or close friends. How you approach the goal of playing golf will vary depending on the values that move you to set that goal.

Whereas a goal is often something that you do or do not obtain, a value is something that you already have. The goal lies outside, in the world, and the value resides in you. Suppose you are a single person with the goal of getting married. You're drawn toward that goal because you value shared experiences, intimacy, and love. As you pursue your goal, it's important to keep sight of the values behind it. Otherwise, it's possible you might obtain your goal of marriage, but with limited shared experience, insufficient intimacy, and not enough love. Not only that, being in touch with your values can guide you to make shared experiences, intimacy, and love part of your life now, even as you continue to pursue the goal of a successful marriage.

Correct or Incorrect

While knowing what your values are is very helpful, it doesn't make sense to say that your values are right or wrong. Answer this question: Which flavor of ice cream do you tend to like better, chocolate or vanilla? Do you know the answer? Okay, now suppose I were to tell you that your answer is wrong. How meaningful would that be? The most it could possibly mean is that my ice cream values and yours are *different*. How can we say that one is right and the other is wrong?

When we try to evaluate what set of values is right or best, we run into a problem. What, exactly, do you use to evaluate what is right or best? Isn't it fair to say that you use your values to do this? Suppose you were to make a list of your values and then evaluate that list. If you decided that there was something important missing from that list, what would that mean? Not about the list, but about *you?* Wouldn't it mean that the missing thing was important to you…that in fact it was a value that could be added to the list of your values? In this way, your values, unlike anything else, are self-contained and uniquely beyond your own judgment. This is another way that our values are a lot like the contextual self. Not only are both of them enduring and stable, they are both separate and distinct from your experience, even your judgments.

Proceeding with Purpose

Clarifying and connecting with your values can help you to make room for uncomfortable feelings and thoughts and to make choices consistent with those values. In our LLAMP acronym, making value-driven choices means *proceeding with purpose*. The problem with most compulsive behaviors and rituals is that even the people who engage in them often find them to be pointless and nonproductive. Think of Judy's complicated rituals surrounding her value-guided attempts to study and prepare for that exam. Governed by the barometer rather the compass, these rituals are *valueless* activities. While they may offer temporary relief from discomfort, compulsive behaviors and rituals actually move us further away from the life we want to live.

Changing our behavior is rarely easy, especially when it means feeling things we do not want to feel. Yet people do difficult things all the time. If you see someone challenging the odds, enduring adversity, and carrying on in spite of hardship, they are likely doing these things because of a value they hold. In most cases, they can tell you exactly what that value is. Having clarity about *why* we are doing a difficult thing creates more space for the difficult feelings and thoughts that come with that choice. Going back to our see-saw metaphor, if anxiety and obsessive thoughts are weighing down one side of the see-saw, being clear about our values is like putting weight on the other side. Our values can act as ballast, tipping us toward acceptance of uncomfortable feelings and an openness to uncertainty.

Values do this, in part, by providing a different *context* for what we are experiencing. In my work with patients who struggle with fear of flying, I've noticed a surprising pattern. The same patient who struggles to endure a three-hour flight that is a required part of a job that they don't particularly care for is likely to have much less trouble on a ten-hour flight that is part of a long-anticipated Parisian vacation. Patients with extreme contamination fears and the most diligent avoidance of other people's germs can make room for much more risk when facing the prospect of physical intimacy with someone they find attractive. When we are focused on the compass and know why we are sailing in a particular direction, we are far more willing to experience the choppy waters that lie in our path.

Clarifying Your Values

We all have values, and much of the time, these values are already guiding our actions and choices. Thinking a bit more about exactly what those values are and articulating them more clearly can help us to align our choices more closely with what is most important to us. Knowing more clearly why we are moving in a specific direction can open us up to the difficult parts of that movement. Developing clarity about what our values are provides a context not only for what we are doing, but also for our experience of doing it. A good first step toward this increased clarity is to think about how you already spend your time. What are the things you are interested in and seem to care about? What exactly is it about those things that is most valuable to you?

Sometimes, we know that we like something, but exactly what we value about it may not be readily apparent to us. Since childhood, I have always been curious about and interested in old buildings. It started with an early fascination with castles, then with older houses and even office buildings in my hometown. As an adult, I never tire of long walks all over San Francisco, taking in its unique Victorian and Edwardian architecture. I've always chosen to live in older buildings, and I tend to seek out and tour historic homes and other structures when I travel. I've spent a lot of time reading about and taking classes on architectural history. Early on, I considered pursuing architecture as a profession but found that I had no real interest in designing anything myself. It took many years for me to recognize and understand exactly what it is about old buildings that I value and care about. For me, these buildings are about people. They say something about the people who built them and lived in them, about how they saw themselves, and how they wanted to be seen by others. I value the connection to earlier generations that older buildings offer us. We're all here for a relatively brief time, and the buildings we live and work in are among the most enduring physical things we leave behind. For me, exploring an older city is like being inside of a huge, collaborative work of art created over multiple generations. The value I place in this is the same one that leads me to listen to the music that my grandparents loved (Guy Lombardo is a favorite) and to collect and transcribe family folklore.

These things offer me a valued sense of connection and continuity with people who were here before me, adding depth and perspective to my own time here. Becoming clearer about the values behind my interest in old buildings has helped me to focus what I do with that interest. Now instead of just enjoying older buildings, I support efforts to preserve them and help others to appreciate them by leading architectural walking tours.

When Anthony looked at his interests and considered how he wished to spend his time, he came up with the following list of core values:

1. Creating and enjoying music and art

2. Intimate connections and shared experiences with others

3. Staying fit and healthy

4. Long-term financial security

To come up with your own list, start by thinking about how you already spend your time. What gets your attention? What do you care about, and why do you care about it?

Shopping at the Values Mall

It might help to complete this values clarification exercise, first published in my book *The Worry Trap*. I've used it with patients for many years as a way to begin a conversation about their values. It's designed to help you think about several different areas of life, assessing which areas are most important to you and what your core values are within those areas:

Welcome to the Values Mall. As you shop at each store in the mall, imagine that each of the experiences or qualities that you buy there will be part of your life going forward. Unfortunately, the ones that you do not buy will be absent from your life. There are seven stores in the mall. In a given store, you can buy as many items as you like, or none at all. However, you have exactly $100 to spend. Keep a running total of how much you have spent, and do not to go over $100. Since the costs of living these values will vary, all of the "prices" in the Values Mall have been randomly assigned. Happy shopping!

Welcome to the Values Mall!

Leisure and Learning Lane	
Traveling	$6
Learning new things	$8
Relaxation and meditation	$7
Enjoying a hobby or sport	$5
Enjoying art, music, or literature	$6

The Family and Friends Store	
Helping loved ones in need	$9
Hanging out and laughing with loved ones	$8
Emotional intimacy and personal sharing	$6
Meeting new people	$7
Belonging to a club or group	$5

The Love Boutique	
Long-term commitment and fidelity	$8
Companionship and shared interests	$5
Physical intimacy and sex	$7
Romance and excitement	$8
Emotional connection with partner	$9

Career-Mart	
Making a lot of money	$8
Doing work that is challenging or creative	$7
Helping others	$8
Flexibility and autonomy	$5
Doing something easy and low-stress	$9

The Spirituality Shop	
Prayer and meditation	$7
Knowledge/understanding of spiritual writings	$7
Believing and practicing a specific religion	$9
Belonging to a spiritual community	$5
Feeling connected to a higher power	$6
Community Corner	
Being politically aware and involved	$8
Volunteering to help others	$6
Protecting the environment	$6
Patriotism	$8
Being ethical and fair	$7
The Mind-Body Connection	
Eating healthy foods	$7
Exercising regularly	$9
Psychological awareness/mental health	$6
Managing stress well	$7
Living as long as possible	$6

Thank you for shopping at the Values Mall. Was it easy to decide what to buy and what to leave behind? Did you have to make some difficult choices? In which stores did you make the most purchases? Where did you make the fewest? What are the values reflected in your choices?

This is a simple exercise, but I think it captures the fact that we have limited time, energy, and resources and often have to choose which areas of life we will focus on and develop. The items within each category, or "store," represent different values that can sometimes pull us in opposing directions. Being clearer about which values are most important to you can help you to make the difficult choices that life often requires of us.

Avoidance, Compulsions, and Values

As you begin to apply the skills presented in this book, letting go of your struggle to control or avoid anxiety and saying yes to your thoughts and feelings, you will have the opportunity to make choices that move you in valued directions. When you're confused about how to proceed, you can apply the Values Test, asking yourself how a given choice adds value to your life. Is this move guided by your compass? Or is it a move away from what you value and guided more by fear? Try to be honest about the cost of avoiding difficult choices and spending time and energy on compulsions and rituals. What might you gain by saying no to valueless compulsions and rituals? What would you have to say yes to in order to move in a valued direction?

Let's look again at Anthony's list of core values:

1. Creating and enjoying music and art

2. Intimate connections and shared experiences with others

3. Staying fit and healthy

4. Long-term financial security

When Anthony looked at the amount of time and energy he put into avoiding possible contaminants like snot and feces, and the cleaning and washing rituals he engaged in, he had to admit that none of these efforts contributed much to the values on his list. In fact, these activities often interfered with his creative efforts and his desire to connect and share experiences with other people. He also acknowledged that throwing away new clothing and shoes as he routinely did when they became "contaminated" undermined his value of financial security to some degree.

When Anthony began to think about looking at and walking near feces as moving toward a more creative and social life, he was able to make room for and accept more discomfort in the interest of those values. When he was able to equate wearing "contaminated" clothing with building more financial security, it became a little easier for him to do so. Most significantly, when he recognized that letting go of a measure of order and control of his personal space actually meant moving toward more intimacy and shared experiences with Lisa, he was finally able to invite her to move in with him. He even cleared out some closet space for her.

In the final chapter of this book, we look at how all of the components of LLAMP can work together to help you tilt toward accepting uncomfortable thoughts and feelings with less struggling and less judgment. As you work to develop these skills, it is important to think about why you are making the effort. If you are able to be more accepting of uncomfortable feelings and spend less time and energy trying to escape or control obsessive thoughts, what will you be doing instead? If acceptance allows for more commitment, what exactly would you like to commit *to?*

CHAPTER 11

Unstuck

We've covered a lot of ground, and now we're heading into the home-stretch. We started with an examination of the fight-or-flight response and how it changes both the content of our thoughts and how we relate to those thoughts. We learned that, as part of this response, cognitive fusion has both helped us to survive and contributed to a wide range of suffering. We identified this increased stickiness between thoughts and what they refer to as key to understanding OCD and Pure O in particular. Along the way, we met six individuals struggling with different types of obsessive thoughts and with avoidant and compulsive responses to those thoughts. Hopefully by now, you are beginning to notice cognitive fusion when it occurs, especially when it leads to a struggle to change or control your thoughts. You may be more aware of the increased stickiness of thoughts when it comes to magical thinking, thoughts about the past or future, and thoughts about your "self."

In the second half of this book, I introduced five steps, or skills, to help you tilt away from your struggle with obsessive thoughts toward a more accepting relationship with them. Practicing and developing these skills means being able to recognize and *Label* sticky thoughts, *Let go* of your struggle to control them, and begin to *Accept* them as separate from the reality that they are an analog of. Being more *Mindful* of the present moment that your thoughts are a part of and connecting more fully with your *Purpose* and values can help you tilt toward more acceptance, flexi-bility, and willingness to take action. In this final chapter, we will look at how these five skills can work together in concert to change the role of obsessive thoughts in your life.

Tilting with LLAMP

ACT is a very flexible approach. Its different components, captured in our LLAMP acronym, can be applied and work together in any number of ways. Depending on your unique challenges and individual preferences, your personal application of these skills may look more like LAM or LAP. It could be as tailored as MAP or PAM, or as streamlined as a simple LA. To illustrate this and address some of the issues that can arise along the way, we'll touch base one more time with Anthony, Sophie, Lou, Judy, Miguel, and Carl. Their individual plans for change, and how they applied the skills presented in this book, offer both hope and a reality check on how this looks in practice. I'll also provide a simple template for structuring your own plan to apply these skills. You'll start by listing specific problems related to your obsessive thoughts, then use that list to generate weekly commitments regarding how you respond to those thoughts. This plan is where the rubber of acceptance meets the road of commitment. First, let's look at how each of the LLAMP skills ultimately came into play for our principal protagonist, Anthony.

The problem that brought Anthony into therapy to begin with was his avoidance of poo on the sidewalk. His efforts to avoid anything suspicious while navigating around the city had become exhausting, and, as I mentioned earlier, he had experienced a dangerously close call when he ran into the street to avoid that portable toilet. Anthony made significant progress on this front early on. He embraced and even came to enjoy our game of taking pictures of increasingly disturbing turds that he encountered throughout the city. He also began to visit and use public bathrooms, rating them using his "five-star" system. Remember learning about exposure and response prevention in the book's introduction? Photographing turds and using and rating public bathrooms was the exposure part. As for response prevention, Anthony was able to reduce and, in some cases, eliminate many of his cleaning rituals. He limited himself to one shower a day and spent less time in the shower. He washed his clothes less often and stopped discarding "contaminated" clothing. He even started to wear that notorious jacket. Anthony was able to do these things, in part, by more accurately *labeling* his experience, noting that he was having "thoughts" of poo or snot. This made it easier for Anthony to more routinely lean into those thoughts, *letting go* of his struggle to control or avoid them. Humor and other defusion methods (part of the *acceptance* move) helped him to grasp that he was leaning into thoughts rather than actual poo or snot. Still, acceptance was very much a tilt. Anthony compared putting on the "snotty" jacket to diving into a cold swimming pool. It involved saying yes to the thoughts of snot the same way he would say yes to the shock of cold water. Accepting "shitty" or "snotty" thoughts by focusing on over-the-top images of rolling around in the stuff only made it clearer that what he was saying yes to were thoughts. What he was experiencing was cognitive defusion. With the jacket, he practiced the *mindfulness* step of rubbing and touching the jacket frequently, noticing that it did not feel particularly snotty in the moment. Finally, he focused on the value, or *purpose,* of being able to move freely about the city, use the bathroom when and where he needed to, and wear more of his clothing.

Exposure and Response Prevention: Anthony and Sophie

Anthony's most significant gains happened later, however, when exposure and response prevention became more clearly connected to his values. This second phase of treatment was prompted by Lisa's request that they finally move in together. Recognizing that moving in with Lisa would "make his life bigger" and move him in a valued direction, Anthony was more willing to lean into the fears that had turned his apartment into a "safe" but isolating bubble. In the month before Lisa was scheduled to move in, he took all of the contaminated clothing that remained at the back of his closet and spread it around his apartment, even rubbing contaminated jeans all over the sheets of his bed and walking all over the apartment in theoretically "shitty" tennis shoes. This was Anthony's "move" toward acceptance, and a vertigo-inducing tilt for him. What he discovered was that "if everything in my apartment is contaminated, it's almost like nothing is contaminated. The contamination becomes more like background noise...or like the paint on the walls." Anthony's ultimate act of letting go was when he committed to not showering for four days and only washing his hands after a bowel movement. When he came in for our session at the end of the four days, his hair was oily and he smelled pretty bad, but he was more relaxed than I had ever seen him.

After Lisa moved in, Anthony had to become even more flexible. After a couple of months, they started having friends over. They did ask their guests to remove their shoes, but as Anthony pointed out, this is standard operating procedure in Japan. Anthony and I ended treatment about this time, but I heard from him again about a year later. He and Lisa were now engaged and had moved into a bigger place. He was sharing a studio space with another artist and making sculpture, some of which he had sold at a local gallery. The biggest news was that Lisa was pregnant. While he was a little anxious about finances, for the most part, Anthony was excited about becoming a dad. The last time I spoke to him, Anthony was leaning into frequent and close contact with a significant amount of poo. Lisa had decided that it was in everyone's best interest for Anthony to be the primary diaper changer in their new family.

As we discussed in the introduction, exposure and response prevention (ERP) has proven to be a very effective approach to treating OCD (Franklin et al. 2000). Behaviorally speaking, the core of Anthony's treatment plan involved both exposure and response prevention. The benefit, however, is the flexibility and skills that he developed along the way. While wearing that infamous jacket, taking pictures of turds, touring public bathrooms, and intentionally "contaminating" his apartment were all exposure for Anthony, doing these things involved *labeling* his thoughts as thoughts, *letting go* and leaning into discomfort, using defusion to facilitate *acceptance*, and being *mindful* of other parts of his experience. Connecting with a *purpose* for doing exposure facilitated all of the other steps. Limiting his handwashing and showering are examples of response prevention and provided more opportunity for doing all of the above. Later, when you think about those weekly commitments that will be part of your personal plan for change, some of them will likely amount to either exposure to triggers or the prevention of your customary response. By following your plan, you'll be practicing the essential elements of ERP. Focusing on making use of and developing the LLAMP skills will help you not only to do what's there to be done now, but to take on similar challenges in the future.

Simply choosing to sit with and lean into obsessive thoughts when they occur can be a form of exposure. This might involve intentionally seeking out TV shows, movies, or books that trigger those thoughts, or even developing your own obsession "scripts" that intentionally capture the most disturbing parts of your obsessive thoughts. Setting aside a specific time each day, you can use the scripts as a starting point to intentionally generate and then lean into obsessive content. You might include these more focused, formal exposures as part of your weekly commitments. Your plan should also include elements of response prevention like not avoiding specific triggers and reducing or skipping compulsions. Whether you use the weekly commitment plan outlined below or a more formally structured program of ERP, the ACT skills included in LLAMP can help you move forward with both the E and the RP of ERP. Let's turn now to Sophie, whose story also included intentional exposure to her obsessive thoughts as well as a committed period of response prevention.

I've never met a sweeter or more sensitive sociopath than Sophie. She initially sought therapy with another provider, looking for a thorough "assessment" to determine if she was indeed a sociopath and to see if therapy could correct this. The other therapist identified Sophie's distress as OCD and referred her to me. The thought part of all of this was very confusing for Sophie at first. How could she know for sure that this was just OCD? What helped was to focus more on the feeling part of her experience initially. Sophie was able to identify two distinct, strong feelings that were part of her distress: fear and love. She felt a strong fear of being a sociopath. This possibility distressed her primarily because of the strong love she felt for her parents much of the time. What bothered Sophie were the moments when she did not feel that love so strongly. It helped Sophie to think of her fear as a reflection of her love. When she did not feel the love, she could tell that it was still there because of her fear. We discussed other ways of *knowing* we love someone even in moments when we don't *feel* that love so strongly. We compared it to knowing that you like ice cream even though you may not want any right now. While Sophie sat with this concept, we agreed to address the fear first, and the love second.

We framed Sophie's fear as a "phobia of an idea." The idea was that she was a sociopath, and overcoming the phobia meant *exposure* to that idea. Sophie had trouble even saying the word "sociopath" initially, but then really embraced a number of the defusion methods described in chapter eight, reducing "sociopath" to "just another word." This allowed her to notice and accept when her mind "went down the socio path." Identifying the part of her mind that questioned her love for her parents as "The Love Police" was a defusion technique that helped Sophie to notice that these thoughts were not *her*, highlighting the two entities of self and experience, which allowed room for relational change. As additional exposure to these thoughts, she agreed to watch several movies about sociopaths, just observing and noting the thoughts and feelings this brought up. She found that when she tried to picture herself playing the role of the sociopath in these movies, it was more humorous than convincing. This was all part of leaning into and letting go of her struggle with the *idea* of being a sociopath and separating this idea from reality.

Elements of both exposure and response prevention were involved in what Sophie and I called the "maybe" game, which targeted Sophie's frequent reassurance-seeking behavior. In this game, Sophie could ask me any question regarding her sociopath status (exposure), and I would reply with a not-so-reassuring "maybe" (response prevention/more exposure). We often found ourselves playing it unexpectedly:

Sophie: Do you think there's any chance I could be a sociopath and I'm just fooling you?

Me: Maybe.

Sophie: Are you just saying that as exposure, because you know I'm seeking reassurance?

Me: Maybe.

Sophie: So I guess this is supposed to help me make room for ambiguity. I can never know absolutely for sure that I'm not a sociopath. There will always be a tiny possibility that I am.

Me: Maybe.

While the fun of this game can be a little one-sided, it's a useful strategy for partners, friends, and family members of people who frequently seek reassurance related to obsessive thoughts. It's important that both parties agree at the outset to the rules of the game, then stick to them.

Sophie was able to give up her "checking" rituals of imagining her parents' funerals pretty easily once she understood how it played into maintaining her obsessions. What was much more difficult to address were the reassuring rituals of calling or texting her parents and repeatedly professing her appreciation and love for them. When I suggested that Sophie stop telling her parents she loved them, her initial reaction was less than enthusiastic: "That's horrible! What kind of therapist *are* you?!"

We finally agreed on a month-long break from saying or writing "I love you" to either of her parents, prefaced by a letter to them that Sophie and I composed together explaining that this was the response prevention part of her treatment and intended to help her be more "emotionally independent."

What surprised us both was how Sophie's parents responded to the letter. They were thrilled with the idea. They sat Sophie down and told her that they both wanted her to be more emotionally independent, not because they didn't love her, but because they did. Also…they wanted to move away. They would both be retiring at the end of the year and were hoping to move to another town that was several hours away. They didn't feel that they could do that until Sophie was more independent and spending more time with her friends than with them. The idea that her parents did not want her to spend more time with them was a revelation to Sophie. All this time, she imagined they were feeling abandoned by her! She went back and forth for a bit between feeling immensely relieved and mildly insulted that her parents wanted more rather than less space in their relationship with her.

When it came to the love part of the equation, it was important for Sophie to make contact with her larger contextual self and the abiding value—love of her parents—that was part of that self. This love was context, and a constant, and was distinct from her *feelings* of love and her day-to-day experience of loving her parents that changed and developed over time. We looked at these changes in terms of human development. How had Sophie's relationship with her parents already changed, from the time she was an infant through early childhood and adolescence? Were there good reasons for this relationship to continue to change and develop as they all aged? Could other people eventually meet some of the emotional needs that her parents met for her now? What would that mean? Would there be moments when she was likely to feel her love for her parents very strongly? How about times when it might be difficult to feel it? This brought us to a discussion of Sophie's beliefs about love. Was it just a feeling like happiness or sadness, or was it something less transitory? Also, was loving someone a zero-sum proposition? If she came to love other people over time, did it mean she would love her parents less? Many of these questions did not have clear answers. We used the Values Test described in chapter ten to help Sophie distinguish between the more stable experience of valuing, or *knowing* she loved her parents, from the more transitory emotional experience of *feeling* love for them. She discovered that it was possible to *know* you love someone, even though you *feel* that love more strongly at some times than at others.

Over time, Sophie became more confident of her love for her parents as an expression of her values rather than as just a feeling she experienced. When they moved away and became more involved in their post-retirement lives, Sophie was more willing to embrace her own busy adult life. She spoke to and visited her parents regularly, and knew that she loved them no matter what she might be thinking about or feeling at a given moment. She was able to laugh at the thought that she could be a sociopath, finally able to appreciate the irony of expressing this thought through tears of concern. Sophie's struggle with the ambiguity of feelings of love and affection came up again, though in a less distressing way, when she got into her first serious romantic relationship. She started to obsess over her feelings, grasping for certainty that she was "in love." The work she had done earlier on separating self from experience and separating love as valuing from love as a feeling served her well in sorting through her feelings in this new context.

A Reality Check: Lou

All the individuals I've introduced here are based on actual patients I've worked with over the years. Their stories offer the opportunity to look at examples of successful strategies as well as some of the challenges that can come up as you're working on your plan and using the skills presented in this book. Being real people, they experienced real outcomes. Steps forward were accompanied by steps back. As I mentioned in the introduction, setting the goal of "overcoming anxiety" is like deciding to stop your brain from doing exactly what it has evolved over millions of years to do. As with anxiety in general, when it comes to living with obsessive thoughts, success is more about significant improvement than about an absolute "cure." To dust off a time-worn but apt trope from the 12-step tradition, it's about "progress, not perfection." Since perfection is a significant part of the problem of obsessive thinking, it makes sense that it would not be part of the solution. Opening yourself up to pain can be very difficult, even when the value of doing so is clear. Often, it takes more than one try. In this way, Lou's story is not unusual and is a good reality check.

At first glance, Lou's obsessive thoughts about his relationship with his son appear to mirror Sophie's concerns about her relationship with her parents. Both of their struggles seem to be triggered by the natural changes that happen even in close relationships as people grow and develop. However, there are important differences. Sophie was triggered by the ambiguity of her own feelings. Lou, on the other hand, was not focused on his own feelings at all, but on what he imagined to be Adam's feelings. And...not the feelings of the Adam he knew and loved, but of a future Adam, who did not yet exist. Lou was experiencing time fusion. He responded to the uncertainty of the future by creating a narrative that included a distant and aloof version of Adam that he experienced as not only real, but fixed and unchangeable. The hallway of Lou's imagination contained only one door, and the future behind it was one of inescapable loss. Not at all hypothetical or speculative as he experienced it, the "realness" of this narrative made it difficult for Lou to participate in and enjoy the present.

The time Lou and I spent together was beset by challenges and is a good example of how therapy can become bogged down and circular. The first challenge was reaching an understanding and agreement about the nature of the problem. Lou had trouble seeing his difficulties as a form of OCD. From his perspective, he was seeking treatment because he was having trouble coming to terms with the inevitability of his son growing distant from him. He wanted help to either feel better about this inevitability or be convinced that it would not be that way. In this framing of Lou's problem, the focus was very much on Lou feeling better. What was left out of the frame was his ongoing avoidance of spending time with his son and the current real-world implications of *that* for their relationship. The OCD formulation would focus our attention on both Lou's thoughts and his response to them. Getting there took quite a lot of work.

When we finally agreed that this was OCD, Lou was able to commit to some specific changes in his behavior. Based on his values around being a parent, he committed to spending time with Adam every evening and going on outings with him every weekend. Lou grasped the concept of cognitive fusion and responded well to the hallway metaphor. He was able to imagine additional doors in that hallway, which represented hope to him. When there were more possibilities, it was easier to see that none of them were real. All of the imagined futures became less sticky. He made good use of defusion methods to tilt toward acceptance of negative narratives as thoughts. I described his use of the "DOOM Radio" exercise earlier. Through labeling, he began to distinguish between "Future Adam" or "Inside Adam" as imaginary and "Present Adam" or "Outside Adam" as real and in need of his attention and presence. Lou also made very good use of the mindfulness step, bringing his attention to Adam and their interactions in the moment. For some reason, Lou found it especially easy to do this when playing with Legos with his son. He referred to this in therapy as "Mindful Legos"—a great example of how mindfulness can come in many forms other than sitting meditation.

In spite of these promising developments, after a brief period of fairly rapid progress, Lou became discouraged again and found new ways to avoid painful feelings and seek reassurance. For a while, things were looking good. Lou was labeling thoughts as thoughts, tilting toward acceptance with defusion exercises, being mindful, and proceeding with purpose on the parenting front. That's the first L and the A, M, P of our LLAMP. What made it difficult for Lou to maintain those gains, it would turn out, was that second L. Lou had great difficulty letting go of his instinctual struggle with negative thoughts when they came up. He was also unwilling to lean into really painful thoughts for any length of time. Because of this, he shied away from using the defusion methods with the new and more disturbing thoughts that came to him, reverting to his old strategy of pushing those thoughts aside. He tended to use mindfulness more as an effort to block out negative thoughts, rather than making room for them along with everything else. Finally, he maintained his commitment to spending time with Adam but betrayed his values as a parent by using that time to seek reassurance from Adam that the two of them would always remain close. He did this by talking to Adam repeatedly about the importance of spending time with one's parents as they aged and noting that many people make a point of living their lives in the same town or even in the same neighborhood as their parents. When an older cousin went off to college, Adam speculated out loud about where he might go to college. When Lou pointed out that there were many good local schools he should consider, Lou's wife insisted that he tell his therapist about the interaction.

At this point, Lou became frustrated with the whole process of treatment and tossed aside the labeling and acceptance tools. He dismissed the fact that they had been helpful. Lou wanted a total cure, and he did not see why it should include feeling painful feelings. He once again questioned the OCD diagnosis, though with less conviction than before. As our sessions began to circle back over the same discussions we had covered at the very beginning of treatment, I also became frustrated. This is when I began to wonder if Lou could benefit from a slightly different approach with another therapist. I know this sounds a bit convenient on my part, and that's not untrue. However, I think it's also a valid and useful conclusion to come to. Sometimes therapy reaches a point where the patient has heard much of what a given therapist has to offer in terms of perspective and tools to address their problems. A fresh perspective and even slightly different tools can give them more to work with. I think it's important to consider this option sooner rather than later, before both patient and therapist start to feel hopeless about the potential for change. I also think it's important for the old therapist and new therapist to collaborate so that there's a sense of continuity and building on that which went before, rather than starting all over.

I referred Lou to a veteran cognitive behavioral therapist who would understand our OCD formulation and the treatment plan that Lou and I had worked through. This therapist did not use an ACT approach but had a lot of experience treating OCD behaviorally with exposure and response prevention. I thought she would be a good fit for Lou, and a change of pace from working with me. She had a reputation for being somewhat "tough" with patients when it came to exposure, where I can be a little soft. The two of us spoke several times about Lou, and I continued to follow his progress, with his permission. In no time, Lou's new therapist had him going to the library with Adam every week to check out books about all the interesting places in the world Adam might someday visit, or where he might even choose to live. After a couple of months, Lou agreed to take Adam on a trip to the East Coast that included "touring" several colleges just to give Adam an idea of the range of options his future might hold. All of this, of course, was exposure for Lou to the idea of Adam one day moving away. It was also, however, a way for Lou to live his values as a parent. While the idea of Adam going out into the world was upsetting for Lou, it was also an option he wanted Adam to have. As Lou's conversations with Adam began to include more questions and answers about other states and cities and education and career paths, Lou began to recognize this as a new way to connect with Adam. Teaching him about the world and exploring possible futures with him was another way to feel close to Adam. It awakened the idea in Lou that he could stay close to Adam by following his journey through life, wherever it took him. The exposure brought in new information that was incompatible with the imagined future that Lou feared. He could now imagine visiting an adult Adam who wanted to share his new home and life with Lou. There were more doors in the hallway. Lou felt less fearful and hopeless about the future and was spending more time with Adam than ever before.

Lou's circuitous path through treatment highlights the obvious fact that different individuals will respond differently to a given treatment approach. Sometimes, taking what seems useful from one approach and then trying something different makes the most sense. It also speaks to the importance of persistence and continuing to work toward change. Avoidance or failure to practice exposure between sessions is a common stumbling block of any behavioral therapy. As evidence-based treatment for OCD becomes more widely available, many areas offer intensive out-patient programs for OCD, which provide more frequent and prolonged sessions that focus exclusively on exposure. Brief stints in programs like these can be an effective supplement to individual therapy for OCD. Participating in an OCD self-help group or connecting with an online community of people struggling with OCD can offer validation, support, and insights that make working on OCD easier and more productive.

Coming Up with a Plan

Whether you're hoping to make some changes on your own or you're working with a therapist, it's important to have a plan. The suggestions in this section offer one way to structure a plan on your own or to play a more active role in developing a plan with your therapist.

As a therapist, the most useful tool I ever picked up is also the simplest: start with a clear *problem list*. I have to give credit for this seemingly obvious strategy to Dr. Jacqueline Persons (1989), whose clear thinking about clinical work has influenced a generation of cognitive behavioral therapists. For nontherapists, this idea of starting with a problem list may not sound so revolutionary. Most people who seek therapy do so because they're having one or more problems. Why wouldn't you start with a list of exactly what these are? Why wouldn't the process of therapy be guided by an attempt to address the problems on this list? Well, I'm not exactly sure, but often it's not. For whatever reason, there is often a lot of talking *around* problems in therapy. Therapy often focuses on descriptions of what's happening currently or in the past and the feelings associated with those events. While these descriptions of events often include components of the relevant problems, that's not the same as spelling out the problem specifically. Sometimes the focus is on a diagnosis and related symptoms that the patient is experiencing. There is certainly a lot of overlap between symptoms and problems, but they're not exactly the same thing. While symptoms often contribute to and are part of a problem, they aren't the whole problem. For example, let's say you were anxious about reaching out to anyone, so you failed to make any plans for the weekend. Spending a weekend alone and feeling sad about it describes what *happened* and how it *felt*, but it doesn't capture the problem. Anxiety about making social plans is a *symptom* of social anxiety, but only part of the problem. It's possible to be anxious and still reach out to others. These incomplete pictures of the problem can lead to therapy that's focused exclusively on feeling less sad or less anxious rather than addressing the actual problem: not reaching out to others when feeling anxious. A clear problem list helps you to target what exactly you want to change. It gives you a "deliverable." If you're working with a therapist, developing a problem list and referring to it regularly can also ensure that you're both working on the same things.

Your Problem List

Start by making a list of things that are problematic or that you would like to change. While your list may seem to include many seemingly unre-lated problems, usually the problems are connected in some way by under-lying elements. When you're done with your list, take a closer look at each problem. Are anxious or obsessive thoughts part of this problem? Does the problem involve some sort of avoidance or compulsive behavior? If any of the problems listed are obsessive thoughts, keep in mind that the problem probably includes more than just the thoughts themselves. The time and energy lost to struggling with thoughts and the avoidance of people, places, or situations because of the thoughts are also important parts of the problem. The same is true of any compulsive behaviors that are a response to thoughts. With this in mind, try organizing the compo-nents of the problems on your list using the following format, which focuses of obsessions and your response to them:

My Problem List

A. Obsessions I Struggle With:

1. _____

2. _____

B. Triggers I Avoid:

1. _____

2. _____

C. Compulsions I Perform:

1. _____

2. _____

As an example, a partial problem list for Anthony might look something like this:

Anthony's Problem List

A. Obsessions I Struggle With:

1. There is poo everywhere

2. Must protect shoes and clothing

B. Triggers I Avoid:

1. Suspicious spots on sidewalk

2. Public restrooms

C. Compulsions I Perform:

1. Looking down while walking

2. Cleaning shoes with antiseptic wipes

Your problem list will help you to spell out which obsessive thoughts, avoidance behaviors, and compulsions are most problematic. If you're working with a therapist, it may be part of a longer, more comprehensive list. You'll likely need to add to this list or make changes over time, as obsessive thoughts have a way of morphing and moving about. As you work toward change, you may also notice more subtle or creative ways of avoiding triggers or new compulsions that crop up. Just add these to your problem list. You will be referring to this list once a week to guide your efforts and keep your plan on track.

Your Commitment List

The next step in creating your plan is to come up with a short list of commitments you're willing to make in the coming week to begin to change how you respond to your obsessive thoughts. These commitments can include sitting with and leaning into thoughts, approaching triggers, and skipping compulsive behaviors when you're triggered. Feel free to start small. Since you'll be making a new commitment list every week, there's no need to try to change everything at once. Try to set yourself up for some early successes by making commitments that seem realistic and attainable at first. For example, instead of skipping a compulsive ritual completely, you can try committing to limiting the time you spend on the ritual, or skipping part of the ritual. You can use the following format for your weekly commitment list:

My Commitment List

    A. *Thoughts to Lean Into:*

        1. _____

        2. _____

    B. *Triggers to Approach:*

        1. _____

        2. _____

    C. *Compulsions to Skip:*

        1. _____

        2. _____

A weekly commitment list for Sophie might look something like this:

Sophie's Commitment List

  A. *Thoughts to Lean Into:*

   1. Maybe I don't really love my parents at all

   2. I might be the best sociopath ever and not even know it

  B. *Triggers to Approach:*

   1. News stories about crimes targeting family members

   2. Watching a movie about a skilled con artist

  C. *Compulsions to Skip:*

   1. Texting parents at bedtime to say goodnight

   2. Calling parents just to say "I love you"

Print out a clear copy of your commitment list and put it someplace you'll see it and can refer to it daily as a reminder of the changes you're working on. Make notes on your success or failure to keep these commitments. Once a week, review your progress. Use your notes and your problem list to generate a new commitment list that feels both relevant and adequately challenging for the coming week. As you get better at keeping certain commitments, you can drop them from the list. For the commitments you're still struggling with, either carry them forward to the coming week or modify them a bit so they're a little easier to take on.

When Obsessions Seem Vague: Judy

While the content of Anthony's and Sophie's obsessive thoughts were very obvious to them, this is not always the case. Sometimes it can be difficult to pin down specifically what thoughts are making you anxious and to put that into words. You may be able to readily identify triggers and the subject matter of obsessive thoughts, but it may take some exploration to identify exactly what it is about an idea that makes you anxious. It may help to ask yourself, *What is it about this idea that I'm really afraid of?* The clearer you are about exactly what the anxiety-producing thought is, the more you'll be able to observe and lean into that thought. Judy initially had trouble identifying the specific nature of the obsessive thoughts that were driving her complicated rituals.

We met Judy briefly in chapter three, on magical thinking. Judy's OCD was fueled by her anxiety about failing or performing poorly academically. Even though she had always done well in school, she lived with the fear that she might fail to do so at any point. Her thinking about this was very black and white. Over time, she had adopted her parents' view that anything less than an A was a failure. When she succeeded in getting into a top-notch university, academics suddenly became more challenging. That's when she started to develop her complex system of rituals to ward off the possibility of failure. Judy suspected at times that these rituals actually interfered with her studying and preparation much more than they helped. This became clearer when I suggested that she try not studying at all and just engage in the rituals the night before an exam. In her more rational moments, Judy was able to acknowledge the lack of connection between her rituals and her grades, but she insisted that they made her *feel* more in control of outcomes.

Unlike the other examples in this book, Judy's OCD does not fall into the category of Pure O. The reason I've included her story is that it demonstrates that the only difference between Pure O and what is more commonly thought of as OCD is the obviousness of the rituals. Judy's rituals are more observable than the avoidance or thought-based rituals seen in our other examples, but other than that, her OCD functions in the same way. Judy is responding to *thoughts* of the possibility of failure the same way she would respond to actual failure. In her experience, controlling these thoughts is the same thing as controlling the possibility of failure. Functionally this is no different from Lou's efforts to control his thoughts about Adam, Sophie's struggle to control thoughts about not loving her parents, or Anthony's moves to control thoughts about poo or snot. For all of these folks, the central problem is an effort to escape or control certain *thoughts*.

Just as it can be difficult for the person with Pure O to recognize the compulsive part of their OCD, it can be hard for someone like Judy to clearly see the obsessive part of the picture. Judy's rituals were so engrossing for her that they effectively distracted her from her thoughts about failing. She was aware of being anxious and that the anxiety was focused on studying and preparing, but initially she had trouble articulating her fears of failure. Early on in treatment, Judy would just say that she was anxious "because I need to study." An important first step toward change for Judy was to observe and articulate the thoughts she was working so hard to avoid. I asked her to tell me what she feared would happen if she didn't study enough. "I might get a bad grade." When I asked what that would mean, she said, "My GPA would suffer. I might not get into graduate school." When I asked why that would be so bad, she said, "I would not get a good job, and my parents would be disappointed in me." When pressed, she went as far as to say, "They might not love me as much." This fused narrative of getting a bad grade, not getting into graduate school, disappointing her parents, and possibly losing their love was the story that Judy was warding off and attempting to control with her rituals. These were the thoughts she would have to make room for and accept as thoughts if she was going to let go of those rituals and focus more on actually studying.

Getting this narrative out in the open and actually writing it down on a piece of paper where Judy could look at it made it easier for her to see it as a story. Whether it seemed realistic or not was not as important as the fact that it made Judy anxious and a little sad. Judy was clear that her rituals were directed at making sure this upsetting story did not come true. What she could not explain was the mechanism by which clock checking and throat clearing could accomplish this. We were able to agree that any connection between the two was "magical." That she was trying to control one thing, over there, by controlling this thing, right here. I suggested the label of "rain dance" to remind Judy of what she was trying to do. Giving up the rain dance would mean being willing to sit with and observe the upsetting story. I emphasized that accepting a story was not the same thing as "buying" that story. Judy hit on the analogy that watching a scary movie about vampires and feeling creeped out by it was not the same thing as believing in vampires. Failing, not getting into graduate school, and losing her parents' love was Judy's vampire movie. It creeped her out, but in the light of day, did not seem all that likely or true.

Because Judy saw herself as a rational person, using the "rain dance" label helped her begin to let go of small parts of her studying rituals. When she noticed anxiety about an upcoming test, she tried to let go of her struggle with it and instead leaned into those anxious feelings. She also made room for her scary narrative about failing and all that it might lead to. She "played the movie" in her head, imagining getting rejection letters from graduate programs and telling her parents about it. She imagined her parents frowning at her and shaking their heads in disgust, then pointing toward the door and banishing her from their home. Judy admitted that as she imagined this last part, it was pretty hard to believe it. Her parents were extremely focused on her success, but she did not doubt their deep love for her. As Judy practiced observing it, this story began to seem a bit contrived or hyped, and a little less scary.

While all of this helped, there was still a lingering connection in Judy's mind between some of her rituals and getting good grades. Before we could move on to more serious response prevention, it was necessary for Judy to get more clarity about her values. While she valued achievement and performing well, she also valued having more time for relaxation and socializing. She was able to see her rituals as very time consuming and not really in service of either of those values. She was also able to acknowledge that even if she aced every exam in college and graduate school and landed her dream job, she would have a hard time enjoying that success if the rituals were still such a big part of her life. How would all of this clock checking and throat clearing go over in a professional environment? Judy understood that she would have to "break the spell" by severing the magical connection between ritual and outcome. To do this, she would have to be willing to risk getting less than an A on at least one test. Together, we made a risk versus risk analysis. Judy weighed the prospect of straight As accompanied by exhausting rituals against the possibility of an occasional B with no rituals.

When Judy was ready to "break the spell," she agreed to do two things the night before her next exam. She removed all clocks from her room, and she made a point of entering her room every time with her left foot (which the OCD told her was the wrong foot). When she had thoughts of failing the exam, she allowed herself to acknowledge those thoughts, "playing the movie" for a moment, and then continuing to study. This wasn't easy for Judy. In fact, she described it as "scary." She did a bit of throat clearing and looking at page numbers, but she also did some belly breathing and a lot of leaning in. The next day, she aced the exam. This paved the way for more studying without rituals, more success, and less fear. She moved on to studying with a clock in the room, at first turned to the wall, then where she could see it, all the while resisting the urge to watch the minute hand. What's important to note is that Judy's anxiety about achievement and even her black-and-white thinking around grades did not completely go away. Over time, however, her relationship to the anxiety and to these thoughts shifted. She was able to recognize that her thoughts were black and white and to make choices that better reflected her values, balancing study time with time for other things.

When Compulsions Seem Vague: Miguel

Unlike Judy, people struggling with "Pure O" OCD more commonly have clearly identifiable obsessive thoughts but more subtle compulsive responses. To see if you fit this pattern, be on the lookout for a propensity for seeking reassurance, either by talking to other people about the thoughts, seeking more information related to the thoughts, or walking yourself through complex arguments for or against certain conclusions. If you struggle with analysis paralysis, sexual orientation obsessions, or relationship OCD, your compulsions may take the form of avoiding decisions, commitments, and taking risks. If this is the case, it might make more sense to start with the list of core values you developed in the last chapter and then identify ways that you fail to act on those values. Your weekly commitment list might involve actions that support commitments and help you embrace choices based on your values. For Miguel, whose obsessions included circular thoughts about changing jobs and committing to versus ending his relationship, learning to distinguish between fear-based and value-based decision making was key.

When I first met Miguel, he had three brand new flat-screen televisions in his living room. They had been there for weeks as he tried to decide which one had the best picture. Miguel liked to have options, and he tended to cling to those options at the expense of living his life. When he was called upon to make a decisive move, he obsessed over his options in an effort to reduce the ambiguity about how each choice might turn out. Since the future is ultimately unknowable, this only increased his anxiety. His compulsive response to this anxiety was to avoid making decisions and, if possible, to hoard more options. Of course, more options only tended to make matters worse. This pattern had kept him in a job he greatly disliked for five years. It had also prevented him from making a lasting commitment to a woman he loved and agreeing to start a family with her.

You'll recall that Miguel was sitting on two equally attractive job offers. Because Miguel experienced the possible futures related to his choices as fixed and predetermined, he believed that his future happiness depended on making the "right" decision. In chapter four, we looked at how this is an example of cognitive fusion. In our work around this decision, I tried to help Miguel see that his future happiness did not depend on the choice he was making now but on his ability to embrace and commit to that choice going forward. Since he had two good opportunities, either one had the potential to work out fine if he applied himself. However, the idea that neither option was clearly better only increased Miguel's anxiety.

Miguel: But if they're both equally good options, how do I know which one to choose?!

This is a clear statement of Miguel's priority of escaping ambiguity. Rather than seeing himself as fortunate to have two good options, he would prefer that one of them be clearly bad. Deciding that one decision must be "right" and the other "wrong" is another attempt to reduce the ambiguity.

Me: If you have two equally good choices, it doesn't matter so much which one you choose. You could probably just flip a coin.

Miguel: Flip a coin?! What kind of therapist *are* you?!

Finally, Miguel thought of something that could tip the scales. Rita was encouraging him to take the offer from the smaller company closer to home. Not having a long commute into the city would fit better with their tentative plan to start a family.

Miguel: If I take that job, it implies I'm signing off on Rita's plan to have a kid, and I'm not ready to decide that yet. So…I should take the job in the city.

So… Miguel was making an important choice based on which option would make it easier for him to avoid making another important choice. In his mind, taking the job in the city left him with more options.

I pointed out that choosing a job that made it easier to have a child in the future was not the same as choosing to have a child. More importantly, this line of thinking amounted to making a decision based on fear. Reminding him of the compass and the barometer, I asked Miguel how his values came into play in making this decision. What was his *purpose* in getting a better job? Why did it matter to him? Miguel came back to two core values that he had expressed before. First, he wanted to be happier at work so he could be happier at home. He was tired of complaining to Rita all the time about his job. Second, he wanted to have a stable job potentially for the next decade so that he could buy a home and maybe start a family. Eventually. Possibly with Rita. Thinking about these values, Miguel observed that Rita was right about the commute making family life harder. If he bought a home, it would likely be in the suburbs. Miguel also thought he might be happier not having a commute. After a little more discussion, he felt that his values were pointing him more clearly toward taking the local job with the smaller company. I pointed out that this values-based decision making did not require Miguel to know the future and how things would turn out. Instead, it was more about knowing himself and what he cared about. This was much more knowable than the future.

Miguel adjusted easily to his new job, and because he wasn't coming into the city any more for work, we met less frequently, then stopped meeting for almost a year. When we did meet again, it had nothing to do with career choices. Miguel was still happy in his new job and had been much happier in his home life with Rita. He was feeling more confident than ever that she was a good partner for him and would be a wonderful mom, should they decide to go that route. Rita, on the other hand, who had just turned thirty-seven, was coming to the end of her rope. She knew that her chances for conceiving a child were about to drop precipitously. When she raised these concerns with Miguel, he made vague references to egg freezing and in vitro as ways to buy more time. Rita pointed out that these offered far from certain outcomes and that the expense involved could easily deplete the down payment they had saved for a house. Finally, Rita told Miguel that it was time to get pregnant or to end their relationship.

Once again, I tried to help Miguel focus on his values rather than his fears. He was clear both that he loved Rita and that he wanted to have a family. What was frightening to him was the permanence and finality of having a family with Rita. He could still imagine a future self that felt limited and trapped by this decision. It turns out, Miguel had some very specific ideas about what he might be giving up. While he still thought about all those women "in the city" that he might date, he was clear that he wasn't up for a lot of dating at this stage of his life. It was just that somewhere among all those women was a (sort of) specific woman he had always imagined he would marry. Unlike Rita, who was dark haired, this woman was blonde. And unlike Rita, who was rather practical and serious, this woman was more "whimsical" and playful. Miguel could see her in his mind's eye this blonde, whimsical wife. Let me be clear. Miguel had never met this woman. While he saw women who looked like her occasionally, out in public, this specific woman was completely made up. In Miguel's fused thoughts of her, however, she existed, waiting for him behind one of the doors in his unlived future. If he fully committed to building a life with Rita, that door, along with the whimsical wife behind it, would be lost to him forever.

Miguel was paralyzed because of two fused thoughts. One was of the whimsical wife who only existed as long as he kept his options open. The other was of his future self, married to Rita and feeling trapped and resentful. For Miguel, losing the first of these meant becoming the second. What was difficult for him to see, because of his anxiety, was that neither of these was real. What was also difficult for him to see was that the costs of buying these thoughts *was* real. In exchange for holding onto this imaginary blonde, whimsical wife, he was about to lose a real, dark-haired, practical woman he deeply loved. Holding onto the possibility of a future that existed solely in the realm of thoughts, he was failing to create a real future and a real child with the real woman that he shared a real and happy history with.

Miguel and I had worked with the hallway metaphor in the past, and I used it now to emphasize the consequences of his remaining in the hallway, both the real-life losses he was about to incur and the imaginary rewards. We used a range of defusion methods, most based on imagery, to help Miguel recognize both his trapped future self and the whimsical wife as phantoms of thought. The defusion made it easier for Miguel to begin labeling both of these images as "made up." He practiced leaning into and accepting them as just images. At the same time, we worked to refocus Miguel on what he valued about his life with Rita, which turned out to be a lot. We also took a hard look at what Miguel's failure to accept uncertainty and make decisive moves based on his values had already cost him and Rita. We were able to use his earlier experience of committing to his current job as an example of how quickly imagined options evaporate and fade next to actualized options that fill our days with their reality. The combination of focusing on what he valued in the real experience of his life with Rita and defusing that sticky narrative of the whimsical wife helped Miguel to take a leap with Rita across the uncertainty and into a future they could build together. In less than a month, he agreed to start trying for a baby with Rita, and the two of them set a date for a small wedding that would be practical but would include a strong element of whimsy as well.

When Values Are Expressed as Fear: Carl

Keep in mind that sometimes values and fear can become confused. This can be especially true when they both point us in the same direction, as when we obsessively fear doing something that contradicts our values. The paradox in this is that in these cases, the fear is offering us some information about our values. This was particularly clear in Sophie's case, where her anxiety about not loving her parents only demonstrated how important loving them was to her. When this is the case, it's important to make some distinction between what is a value and what is fear. For Carl, his concern about being respectful toward women was a value, but it showed up as an obsessive fear that he would violate that value. His compulsive avoidance of certain interactions with women was an expression of the fear, not an expression of the values behind it.

What's really hard about working with people like Carl, who are obsessed with their thoughts about harming others, is how gentle and kind they tend to be. The heightened concern about the welfare of others that fuels their OCD is also visible in their exceptionally caring and sensitive characters. To watch someone like this struggling with the fear that they are secretly a bad, horrible person can be painful. Carl was absolutely meticulous in his concern for the feelings and rights of other people. He had fallen in love with and married a strong, independent woman whom he greatly admired, and he supported her in all of her endeavors. He was a loving father, who encouraged his daughter to fearlessly follow her dreams and insist on the respect of others, especially boys and men. These were core values for Carl. They were also a focus of his anxiety. Like Sophie's fears that reflected her strong love for her parents, Carl's obsessive thoughts were a reflection of his deeply held respect for women. A reflection, however, is not the same thing as that which it reflects. The challenge for Carl was being able to recognize the difference between his values and his fears.

The most important step toward letting go of the struggle with "harm OCD" is also the first one: accurate *labeling* of what is going on. It was essential that Carl understand his experience as OCD and recognize his thoughts as warning signals from his brain, rather than wishes or desires. To get there, it helped for him to read Lee Baer's (2001) short book *The Imp of the Mind*, which does a great job of explaining harm-based obsessions and offers many examples of individuals struggling with them. Their stories make it clear that these are not bad people who wish anyone harm.

Labeling his thoughts as "warnings," like thoughts about falling that come up when we are in a high place, made it easier for Carl to *let go* of his instinct to struggle with these thoughts. Using deep breathing and relaxing his hands, he was able to sit with the thoughts for increasing periods, which made room for practicing other skills. He also used the defusing tactic of thanking his mind for the thoughts, which helped him to observe them as a reflection of his values, even as he noted that these warnings were "louder" than they needed to be.

Once Carl gained a little relief through *labeling* and *letting go*, we skipped forward to look at the *purpose* reflected in his thoughts. Carl already had a lot of clarity about his values around respecting women and gaining consent in sexual interactions. What he needed was help understanding these values as an enduring and central element of who he was as a person. They were part of his true *self*. We worked toward this by observing that these values were not new for Carl. While the cultural awakening surrounding the #MeToo movement had brought them into focus, these values had been present and guiding Carl throughout his life. Everything he could recall from his past indicated that those values had been present and operating.

What bothered Carl, however, was what he could not remember about his past. It was helpful for Carl to note that there were lots of details from his distant past that he could not remember, not just about sexual interactions, but about all sorts of things. However, Carl had fairly clear memories of important or upsetting events from his past. This is how memory works. We tend to remember that which is important or exceptional. Since these values had consistently guided Carl in his choices, any departure from them would have been exceptional, and would be more likely to be remembered. The Jekyll and Hyde notion that people go around committing harmful acts then forgetting that they have committed those acts is a myth. It's the stuff of B movies and comic books, and totally absent from the annals of real-life events. The fact that we do not remember everything, however, lends an element of ambiguity to the past. It's that unknown thing in the bushes. Since the anxious brain does not like ambiguity, it can generate a range of "what if…" scenarios to fill in these gaps in information. Because of cognitive fusion, these imagined scenarios can feel surprisingly plausible. The remarkable thing about imagination is that we can imagine *anything*. Not only that, we can imagine *wanting* or *enjoying* anything. Remember my example of imagining licking the wall and enjoying it? Thoughts of licking the wall does not a wall-licker make.

To tilt toward acceptance of his thoughts as just thoughts, Carl used several of the same defusion methods that Sophie employed, saying the word "rapist" out loud and in different voices to reduce its stickiness. He also allowed himself to observe the imagined scenarios of his "self" spiking women's drinks and forcing himself on them. It was helpful for Carl to notice that he did not enjoy these images. He used the label "not me" as a reminder that the "self" he was observing was not, in fact, him. When he noticed these thoughts of harm coming up when he was around women, he let go of any struggle to control them and brought in more information about the reality of those moments by being mindful of everything else he was aware of. This included his awareness of feelings of attraction toward women as well as his respect for them and enjoyment of interacting with them socially.

Behaviorally, it was important for Carl to be aware of any avoidance or other changes in his interactions with women that were a response to his obsessive thoughts and fear. While he was not actively avoiding spending time with attractive women, he agreed to be more proactive in this area by seeking out interactions with female coworkers and friends whom he found attractive. He suggested to his wife that they have Megan and her husband over for brunch, and made a point of handling Megan's drink. He noticed the thoughts that inevitably came up of spiking that drink and practiced observing and accepting these as thoughts. What Carl noticed, almost right away, was that the more he acknowledged and made room for these thoughts, and the less he struggled to get rid of them, the less he was bothered by them. Refocusing his attention on interacting with the women in his life, guided as he always had been by his values, made it easier to recognize that the person in his "what if..." scenarios was not him. Seeing his anxious thoughts as a reflection of those values made it easier to accept them, thanking his mind for the warning, but knowing that his values had it covered.

Moving Forward with Your Thoughts

I hope you've found this book both enlightening and helpful in a practical way. I've tried to offer a sense of the various forms that OCD can take, especially those Pure O patterns where the compulsive component of the OCD is harder to spot. My hope is that by recognizing formerly "invisible" responses like avoidance or cognitive rituals as key to maintaining obsessive thinking, you will be able to make a clearer commitment to change. I know that "cognitive fusion" has rung out as a sort of refrain in the book. This is a reflection of its central role in OCD. I've tried to demonstrate how it comes into play not just in triggering struggles to control thoughts but in magical thinking, how we think about the past and the future, and even how we think about ourselves.

Whether you are working toward change on your own or with the help of a therapist, I hope that the five skills presented in the second half of the book offer a path toward creating that change. If you're working on a program of exposure and response prevention, these skills can help you to approach that work with more openness and less "white-knuckling." If you would like to read more about any of the five skills presented here, I'll refer you to my earlier book, *The Worry Trap* (LeJeune 2007). While I've made an effort to not repeat content here, that book is also organized around the LLAMP set of tools. Because it's more of a "workbook" than this book is, it offers more examples and exercises for developing each of the tools. Finally, in introducing the six individuals whose stories I've shared here, I hoped to offer a flavor for different forms of Pure O and to illustrate the five skills in action. It was also my wish that Anthony, Sophie, and friends could offer a sense of companionship on your journey through these pages. I wish you all the best as you continue on your way.

Acknowledgments

The ideas, tools, and stories in these pages were collected over many years and came from many different people. The conceptual bones of this book owe much to the imagination, clear thinking, and diligent research of Steven C. Hayes and the co-creators of ACT. From my earliest days working with patients, I found in ACT an elegant and powerful way of approaching the most intimate elements of human experience...our thoughts, feelings, and choices. As a model, it's as flexible as it is coherent. It has come to be my stock-in-trade.

My understanding of anxiety and the many forms that it can take was largely shaped by the research and writing of David H. Barlow. Early books by Jeffrey Schwartz, Lee Baer, and Edna Foa were my "OCD Trifecta," opening my eyes to the nuances of OCD and informing all of my treatment planning. I had the opportunity to make OCD a focus of my clinical work during four formative years at the San Francisco Bay Area Center for Cognitive Therapy. There, Jaqueline Persons shared generously of her expertise and bolstered my confidence. She is a teacher and mentor second to none.

There would be no book here without the many patients who have honored me by sharing both their struggles and their triumphs over the years. The brave individuals I have come to know through my clinical work, their trust, and our collaboration are the most treasured gifts of my professional life.

I am very grateful for the vision and dedication of Matthew McKay, founder of New Harbinger Publications, who supported the publication of my first book, *The Worry Trap*. His personal mission to spread the word, not just of ACT, but of evidence-based healing in general, has helped countless people. My editors at New Harbinger, Caleb Beckwith, Rona Bernstein, and Jess O'Brien have shown tremendous faith in the current book and offered extremely helpful feedback and suggestions.

The decision to finally write this book came about in the midst of a global pandemic, and immediately after the death of my mom. It was a time for circling the wagons, and the most important support was very personal. My partner Warren Box has been a steady, reliable source of love and encouragement day in and day out. Family members like Christopher LeJeune, Geneva Billups, and Karen Quebodeaux Thibodeaux and old friends like Pete Morones and Rhonda Dunaway were palpably and consistently there for me. My dear friend and colleague Tracy Lewellen has been both a rock of support personally and a trusted sounding board for this project. From our discussions of my earliest ideas for the book to reading the first completed draft, her contribution has been indispensable.

References

Alcott, Hunt, Luca Braghieri, Sarah Eichmeyer, and Matthew Gertzkow. 2020. "The Welfare Effects of Social Media." *American Economic Review* 110, no. 3: 629–76.

Attardo, Salvatore. 2017. *The Routledge Handbook of Language and Humor.* New York: Routledge.

Baer, Lee. 2001. *The Imp of the Mind.* New York: Penguin.

Dass, Ram. 1971. *Be Here Now.* New York: Crown.

Eddington, Arthur S. 1929. *The Nature of the Physical World.* New York: Macmillan.

Franklin, Martin E., Jonathan S. Abramowitz, Michael J. Kozak, Jill T. Levitt, and Edna B. Foa. 2000. "Effectiveness of Exposure and Ritual Prevention for Obsessive-Compulsive Disorder: Randomized Compared with Non-randomized Samples." *Journal of Consulting and Clinical Psychology* 68, no. 4: 594–602.

Hayes, Steven C. 2019. *A Liberated Mind: How to Pivot Toward What Matters.* New York: Avery.

Hayes, Steven C., Kirk D. Strosahl, and Kelly G. Wilson. 1999. *Acceptance and Commitment Therapy: An Experiential Approach to Behavior Change.* New York: The Guilford Press.

Homans, George. 1941. "Anxiety and Ritual: The Theories of Malinowski and Radcliffe-Brown." *American Anthropologist* 43: 164–172.

Jaynes, Julian. 1976. *The Origins of Consciousness in the Breakdown of the Bicameral Mind.* Boston: Houghton Mifflin.

Keles, Betul, Niall McCrae, and Annmarie Grealish. 2020.
"A Systematic Review: The Influence of Social Media on
Depression, Anxiety, and Psychological Distress in Adolescents."
International Journal of Adolescents and Youth 25, no. 1: 79–93.

Korzybski, Alfred. 1933. *Science and Sanity: An Introduction to
Non-Aristotelian Systems and General Semantics.* The
International Non-Aristotelian Library Publishing Co.

LeJeune, Chad. 2007. *The Worry Trap: How to Free Yourself from
Worry and Anxiety Using Acceptance and Commitment Therapy.*
Oakland: New Harbinger.

Miller, Andrew. 2020. *On Not Being Someone Else: Tales of Our
Unled Lives.* Cambridge: Harvard University Press.

Persons, Jacqueline B. 1989. *Cognitive Therapy in Practice: A Case
Formulation Approach.* New York: Norton.

Pinker, Steven. 2007. *The Stuff of Thought: Language as a Window
Into Human Nature.* New York: Penguin.

Schwartz, Barry. 2004. *The Paradox of Choice: Why More Is Less.*
New York: Ecco/HarperCollins Publishing.

Schwartz, Barry, Andrew Ward, John Monterosso, Sonya Lyubomirsky,
Katharine White, and Darrin Lehman. 2002. "Maximizing versus
Satisficing: Happiness Is a Matter of Choice." *Journal of Personality
and Social Psychology* 83, no. 5: 1178–1197.

Schwartz, Jeffrey M. 1997. *Brain Lock: Free Yourself from Obsessive-
Compulsive Behavior.* New York: Harper Perennial.

Chad LeJeune, PhD, is a clinical psychologist, and professor of psychology at the University of San Francisco. He is a founding fellow of the Academy of Cognitive and Behavioral Therapies. He has been a practitioner of acceptance and commitment therapy (ACT) since its inception in the early 1990s. He is author of *The Worry Trap*.

MORE BOOKS from
NEW HARBINGER PUBLICATIONS

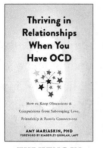
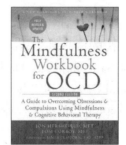

FROM OUR COFOUNDER—

As cofounder of New Harbinger and a clinical psychologist since 1978, I know that emotional problems are best helped with evidence-based therapies. These are the treatments derived from scientific research (randomized controlled trials) that show what works. Whether these treatments are delivered by trained clinicians or found in a self-help book, they are designed to provide you with proven strategies to overcome your problem.

Therapies that aren't evidence-based—whether offered by clinicians or in books—are much less likely to help. In fact, therapies that aren't guided by science may not help you at all. That's why this New Harbinger book is based on scientific evidence that the treatment can relieve emotional pain.

This is important: if this book isn't enough, and you need the help of a skilled therapist, use the following resources to find a clinician trained in the evidence-based protocols appropriate for your problem. And if you need more support—a community that understands what you're going through and can show you ways to cope—resources for that are provided below, as well.

Real help is available for the problems you have been struggling with. The skills you can learn from evidence-based therapies will change your life.

Matthew McKay, PhD
Cofounder, New Harbinger Publications

If you need a therapist, the following organization can help you find a therapist trained in acceptance and commitment therapy (ACT).

Association for Contextual Behavioral Science (ACBS)
please visit www.contextualscience.org and click on Find an ACT Therapist.

For additional support for patients, family, and friends, please contact the following:

International OCD Foundation (IOCDF)
Visit www.ocfoundation.org

Did you know there are **free tools** you can download for this book?

Free tools are things like **worksheets, guided meditation exercises**, and **more** that will help you get the most out of your book.

You can download free tools for this book— whether you bought or borrowed it, in any format, from any source—from the New Harbinger website. All you need is a NewHarbinger.com account. Just use the URL provided in this book to view the free tools that are available for it. Then, click on the "download" button for the free tool you want, and follow the prompts that appear to log in to your NewHarbinger.com account and download the material.

You can also save the free tools for this book to your **Free Tools Library** so you can access them again anytime, just by logging in to your account! Just look for this button on the book's free tools page.

+ Save this to my free tools library

If you need help accessing or downloading free tools, visit **newharbinger.com/faq** or contact us at **customerservice@newharbinger.com**.